The Merrill Studies
in
The Bridge

CHARLES E. MERRILL STUDIES

Under the General Editorship of
Matthew J. Bruccoli and Joseph Katz

The Merrill Studies
in
The Bridge

Compiled by

David R. Clark
University of Massachusetts

Charles E. Merrill Publishing Company
A Bell & Howell Company
Columbus, Ohio

Grateful acknowledgment is made to Liveright Publishing Corp. for permission to quote from *The Complete Poems and Selected Letters and Prose of Hart Crane*, edited with an introduction by Brom Weber, copyright © 1933, 1958, 1966 by Liveright Publishing Corp.

ISBN: 0-675-09292-2

Library of Congress Catalog Number: 70-128783

1 2 3 4 5 6 7 8 9 10—79 78 77 76 75 74 73 72 71 70

Printed in the United States of America

Preface

Although its reputation was immediately controversial, the appearance of *The Bridge* by Hart Crane (1899-1932) clearly placed him in the very first rank of twentieth-century American poets. *The Bridge* was much more ambitious in its scope and attempted unity than was Crane's earlier *White Buildings* (New York: Boni & Liveright, 1926), a collection of lyrics which sympathetic writers had hailed as an event of the first order in the history of American poetry.

A single poem in eight long sections, aiming, as Crane had announced, to enunciate through the symbol of the Brooklyn Bridge "a new cultural synthesis of values in terms of our America,"[1] *The Bridge* was published in a limited edition by the Black Sun Press, Paris, in January 1930, and in a trade edition by Horace Liveright, New York, in October 1930. Its reception was mixed. In essays reprinted here, Malcolm Cowley noted that although the poem "has succeeded to an impressive degree" (in creating "the myth of America"), "the faults are obvious"; Yvor Winters found "many magnificent fragments" in the poem, but deplored Crane's trying to get anywhere with "the Whitmanian inspiration"; Allen Tate commented on "the fragmentary and often unintelligible framework of the poem," finding it only "a collection of lyrics," even though the best of these "are not surpassed by anything in Amer-

---

[1] Brom Weber, ed. *The Letters of Hart Crane* (Berkeley: University of California Press, 1952), p. 223. Copyright 1952 by Brom Weber. This and all other quotations from *The Letters of Hart Crane* used by permission of the publisher.

ican literature"; and other critics praised the success or attacked the faults without unanimity. During the 30s and 40s, most critics echoed Tate's judgment that *The Bridge* is a magnificent failure. Often this failure—especially after Crane's suicide in 1932—was linked with the tragedy of his personal life. In a classic expression of this view Brewster Ghiselin found *The Bridge* a "Bridge into the Sea."

Such comments are not out of tune with Crane's own occasional disillusionment while struggling for seven years with his poem. In a letter of June 20, 1926, just before a creative period in which he wrote some of the grandest and most affirmative poetry of *The Bridge*, he confessed that "The form of my poem rises out of a past that so overwhelms the present with its worth and vision that I'm at a loss to explain my delusion that there exist any real links between that past and a future destiny worthy of it. . . . The bridge as a symbol today has no significance beyond an economical approach to shorter hours, quicker lunches, behaviorism and toothpicks."[2] Yet by August 3rd he was full of enthusiasm. "I feel as though I were dancing on dynamite these days—so absolute and elaborated has become the conception. All sections moving forward now at once!"[3]

During the 50s and early 60s criticism increasingly recognized the degree of artistic unity which Crane had achieved. Here are gathered some of the most significant of these critical essays. Stanley K. Coffman, Jr. helped to turn the tide with an essay on Crane's brilliant use of symbolist technique. John Willingham defended Crane against the charge that the "Three Songs" are "inorganic or inappropriately placed" in relation to other sections of *The Bridge*. L. S. Dembo argued impressively for "The Unfractioned Idiom of Hart Crane's *The Bridge*" in a May 1955 essay in *American Literature*, and then expanded into a book, *Hart Crane's Sanskrit Charge*, his thesis of the unity and wholeness of Crane's poem. John Unterecker called further attention to the "linking devices" which counteract the "superficial fragmentation."

Growing more confident of Crane's achievement, authors of a number of recent books and articles have held the whole poem or parts of it up to increasingly close examination. One of the most illuminating readings is Glauco Cambon's analysis of "Ave Maria" from a fine long essay. In the final essay of this collection, Alan Trachtenberg has assimilated much of the recent criticism of *The*

---

[2] *Ibid.*, p. 261.
[3] *Ibid.*, p. 270.

Bridge, has related the poem firmly but briefly to Crane's life and to his other work, and sees the poem newly as a design in itself and in relation to the social and cultural context behind it.

Cranes' own final comments on *The Bridge* would seem to provide more comfort to his later, rather than to his earlier, critics. The published letters do not show that after it was completed he ever shared his early critics' doubt of his poem. In a letter of April 22, 1930, this "roaring boy" mildly asserted, "It is pertinent to suggest, I think, that with more time and familiarity with *The Bridge* you will come to envisage it more as one poem with a clearer and more integrated unity and development than was at first evident. . . . *The Bridge* is at least as complicated in its structure and inferences as *The Wasteland* [sic]—perhaps more so."[4] And on May 22nd, "The poem, as a whole, is, I think, an affirmation of experience, and to that extent is 'positive' rather than 'negative' in the sense that *The Waste Land* is negative."[5]

---

[4] *Ibid.,* p. 350.
[5] *Ibid.,* p. 351.

Contents

The Merrill Studies
in
The Bridge

Horace Gregory

Far Beyond Our Consciousness

The business of living in any large modern city produces an effect analogous to shell-shock. The screaming of automobile sirens, the winking glare of animated electric signs, the steady roar of the elevated and the subway are imbedded in your flesh. Given an emotional crisis and all these sensations, already more than your senses can bear, create an illusion of penetrating the fourth dimension. Each sensation now carries with it the impact of past experiences and historical associations take on new meaning. Your emotions may not be clearly defined, but they are actual; a kind of religious exaltation touches you as well as terror and for the moment you cannot escape.

It is this particular emotional crisis that arises in Hart Crane's present volume, "The Bridge." But the experience that he gives you is by no means direct. It has been translated into esoteric speech, recreated out of a submerged and literary Anglo-American tradition. In a sense, we have been well prepared for receiving "The Bridge" as one of the latest developments in American poetry. Since the publication of Hart Crane's first book of poems,

From *Books, New York Herald and Tribune,* April 20, 1930, p. 4. Reprinted by permission of Book World.

1

"White Buildings," there has been no small attention given to a revival of interest in metaphysical poetry. Perhaps Hart Crane himself has been partly responsible (within limited circles to be sure) for this revival. His early work is a remarkable mosaic of the vocabularies uttered by John Donne and Herman Melville, united by a centrifugal force that is quite his own. A measure of literary sophistication was necessary for an understanding of Hart Crane's fugitive poems, yet their content closely examined was strictly (and the same holds true in this new volume) non-intellectual. The emotional content is all-important; an attempt to rationalize Hart Crane's images would place them in a false light.

The value of "The Bridge" rests largely upon Hart Crane's ability to break away from the tendencies indicated by his immediate predecessors. T. S. Eliot had struck the dominant note for an entire movement. His approach to the contemporary scene was one of exact analysis. He showed you our cities, top heavy with skyscrapers and millions of people, crowding, driving the highly sensitized individual into a corner. The individual became a spectator, bitterly commenting upon a waste land, searching out the precise nature of the spectacle before him, quite as a scientist may attempt to reconstruct the character of a butterfly by the minute inspection of one of the creature's legs under the powerful lens of a microscope.

Not so Hart Crane. The analysis of what is set before him is incidental. He sees an image of the bridge springing from a remote past and propelled upward, spiraling, arching the sky, casting its shadow down upon us and vanishing in space. Opening with an invocation to Brooklyn Bridge, the poem leaps forward. The bridge is at once a road and an intangible thoroughfare on which our memories and dreams progress forever, reaching far beyond our consciousness.

Columbus, for an instant only, rises from Genoa:

> The sea's green crying towers a-sway, Beyond
>
> And kingdoms
> > naked in the
> > > trembling heart—
> > Te Deum laudamus
> > > O Thou Hand of Fire.

And the poem speeds onward across the North American continent and back again piercing time and space. Here lies Ohio and there New England. "Perennial-*Cutty*-trophied-*Sark*" revivifies the Pacific and Atlantic harbors. The river, the Mississippi flows, "Meeting the Gulf, hosannas silently below." Pocahontas dances again and the violet Adirondacks rest against the sky. Walt Whitman and Cape Hatteras swing into view, then New York and its subways and at last, the bridge vaulted into distance becomes one with the myth of Atlantis.

These are the obvious elements of the poems that by loose association with a central image are bound together for the expression of a genuinely religious point of view. Despite Hart Crane's occasional lapses into rhetoric that becomes merely florid and diffuse there is no one writing poetry today with like emotional intensity. He is an excellent artist, yet he is erratic and prodigal in the use of his talent. There are times when he can be both simple and precise. Here are the closing lines of a division of the poem called "Indiana":

> Come back to Indiana—not too late!
> (Or will you be a ranger to the end?)
> Good-bye . . . Good-bye . . . oh, I shall always wait
> You, Larry, traveller—
> stranger,
> son,
> —my friend—

This spontaneous, lyrical flow of emotion, rising at intervals throughout the poem, always comes upon us as a fresh surprise. The poem has overtones of sadness and despair. "Dark waters onward shake the dark prow free" and

> Now pity steeps the grass and rainbows
> ring
> The serpent with the eagle in the
> leaves. . . ?

are characteristic lines. But here is another passage written with radiant buoyancy and verve for he has enough vitality to supply the life-force of a dozen poets:

> Macadam, gun-grey as the tunny's belt,
> Leaps from Far Rockaway to Golden
> Gate:
> Listen! the miles a hurdy-gurdy grinds—
> Down gold arpeggios mile on mile
> unwinds. . .

Another poem aptly describes the inferno of "The Tunnel," the subway ride from Columbus Circle to Brooklyn:

> Whose head is swinging from the
> swollen strap?
> Whose body smokes along the bitten
> rails,
> Bursts from a smoldering bundle far
> behind
> In back forks of the chasms of the
> brain,—
> Puffs from a riven stump far out behind
> In interborough fissures of the mind. . . ?
> And Death, aloft—gigantically down
> Probing through you—toward me, O
> evermore!
>
> And when they dragged your retching
> flesh,
> Your trembling hands that night
> through Baltimore—
> That last night on the ballot rounds,
> did you
> Shaking, did you deny the ticket, Poe?

In some respects, "The Tunnel" is the most effective section in the poem. As in "Cutty-Sark," Hart Crane's projection of the Atlantic seaboard with all its associations, the structure of the entire poem is sustained. In other sections, the design wavers, leaps into our consciousness and then falls into darkness.

It is impossible to predict a future for Hart Crane. With the publication of "The Bridge" his promise as an important American poet is fulfilled. His defects and merits are here, eloquently displayed. His effort to create a synthesis (himself deeply affected by the disintegrating forces that mark the work of his contemporaries) is a notable contribution to American poetry.

Malcolm Cowley

A Preface to Hart Crane

"The poetry of Hart Crane is ambitious," said Allen Tate at the beginning of his valuable introduction to *White Buildings*. Four years later, in reviewing Crane's second book of poems, I can only make the statement again, but this time for a different reason. The ambitiousness of his earlier work was shown partly in tone, in its assumption of the grand manner, and partly in its attempt to crowd more images into each poem—more symbols, perceptions and implications—than any few stanzas could hold or convey. The result in some cases was a sort of poetic shorthand which even the most attentive readers could understand with difficulty. In this second volume, merely by making the poems longer, he has made them vastly more intelligible. His ambition, which has grown with his achievement, is now shown in his choice of subject.

The Bridge is a unified group of fifteen poems dealing primarily with Brooklyn Bridge. But the bridge itself is treated as a symbol:

From *Think Back on Us . . . A Contemporary Chronicle of the 1930's*, ed. Henry Dan Piper (Carbondale and Edwardsville: Southern Illinois University Press; London and Amsterdam: Feffer & Simons, Inc., 1967), pp. 199-202. Copyright © 1967 by Southern Illinois University Press. Reprinted by permission of Southern Illinois University Press. First appeared in *The New Republic*, LXII (April 23, 1930), 276-77.

it is the bridge between past and future, between Europe and the Indies; it is the visible token of the American continent. And, although this book of poems—this one massive poem divided into eight sections and fifteen chants—begins with a modest apostrophe to a bridge over the East River, it ends bravely as an attempt to create the myth of America.

We might well conclude that such an attempt was foredoomed to failure. An ambitious subject is by definition a subject rich in platitudes; nor is this its only danger. A poet who chooses such a theme and who, by power of imagination or intensity of feeling, escapes the platitudinous, is tempted to assume the role of a messiah. Many ambitious poems are both messianic and commonplace, but *The Bridge*, I think, is neither. In its presumptuous effort the poem has succeeded—not wholly, of course, for its faults are obvious; but still it has succeeded to an impressive degree.

The faults of *The Bridge* I shall leave to other reviewers. As for the causes of its artistic success, they are not mysterious; they are complicated. They depend on the structure of the volume as a whole, which in turn is too elaborate, too much a fabric of interwoven strands, to be explained in the present review. Instead of advancing a few vague statements, I prefer to suggest Crane's general method by describing in detail one of the fifteen poems. But which? . . . The poem that suggests itself is possibly his best; probably it is one of the important poems of our age, but it is not immeasurably better than others in the book—"Cutty Sark," for example, or "The Dance," or "Ave Maria"—and its method is neither too simple nor too complex to be typical of his work. Let us confine ourselves, then, to "The River."

It occurs in the second section of the book, a section bearing the name of Pocahontas, whom the poet has chosen as an earth-symbol to represent the body of the American continent. She also represents its Indian past. The section dedicated to her consists of five poems, each of which progresses farther into the continent and into the past, till the Indian tradition fuses, in the fifth poem, with that of the settlers. It should be noted, however, that the progression is not geographical or historical: it is a progressive exploration of the poet's mind. Thus, in the first poem of the series, he awakens to the dim sounds of the harbor at dawn; in the second he walks to the subway attended by the imaginary figure of Rip Van Winkle. In the fourth poem, he will picture a corn-dance held by the Indians before the first settlers landed on the marshy banks of the James. The third poem, with which we are dealing to the exclusion of the others, must serve as a link between the second and the fourth—between present and past, between New York City and the Appalachian tribes. Thus, it must have a movement both temporal and spatial, a movement like that of a river; and the subject Crane has chosen to perform this double function is the Mississippi.

His treatment of the subject is oblique; he does not proceed logically, but rather by associations of thought, by successive emotions. Since the preceding poem has ended in a subway, it seems emotionally fitting to begin the present one, not on the Mississippi itself, but on a train westbound from Manhattan into the heart of the continent. From the windows of the Twentieth Century Limited, the poet watches the billboards drifting past. And the first eighteen lines of this long poem are a phantasmagoria of pictures and slogans, an insane commentary on modern life, an unstable world as seen in glimpses by a moving observer.

Suddenly the angle of vision changes. The poet is no longer on the train; he is standing beside three ragged men "still hungry on the tracks . . . watching the taillights wizen." The rhythm of the poem changes at the same moment: it is no longer nervous and disconnected; it settles down to the steady pedestrian gait of hoboes plodding along a railroad. The next ninety-three lines, by far the longest section of the poem, will deal with the Odyssey of these unshaven men, "wifeless or runaway," of whom Crane once said in explaining his methods: "They are the leftovers of the pioneers. . . . Abstractly, their wanderings carry the reader through certain experiences roughly parallel to those of the traders and adventurers, Boone and others."

From the long passage that deals with these wanderings, I remember many lines, some for their vividness or wit, some for their music, and some for the imaginative quality that is poetry in the strictest sense:

> *"There's no place like Booneville though, Buddy,"*
> *One said, excising a last burr from his vest,*
> *"—For early trouting." . . .*

> *John, Jake or Charley, hopping the slow freight*
> *—Memphis to Tallahassee—riding the rods,*
> *Blind fists of nothing, humpty-dumpty clods. . . .*

> *—They know a body under the wide rain;*
> *Youngsters with eyes like fjords, old reprobates*
> *With racetrack jargon,—dotting immensity*
> *They lurk across her, knowing her yonder breast*
> *Snow-silvered, sumac-stained or smoky blue—*

Lurking across immensity, they wander wherever the Mississippi "drinks the farthest dale." In Ohio, "behind my father's cannery works," they squat in a circle beside the tracks. They remember "the last bear, shot drinking in the Dakotas." Drifting through the Missouri highlands, they linger where—

> *Under the Ozarks, domed by Iron Mountain,*
> *The old gods of the rain lie wrapped in pools*

and inevitably they gather at Cairo, where the waters gather. "For," says the poet addressing these belated pioneers—"For you, too, feed the River timelessly." The poem, after wandering over half the country, has found its proper subject. And at this point the rhythm changes once more; it becomes slower, more liquid; and finally, in a series of eight majestic quatrains, the river and the poem flow southward together, passing De Soto's burying place, passing "the City storied of three thrones," and mingling with the Gulf.

Even from this bare outline of one poem, one can glimpse the qualities by which the ambition of the volume is transformed into realization. Here is the conceptual imagination that resolves a general subject into an individual experience—one which it again dissolves into something universal and timeless. Here is the concrete imagination that reveals itself in terms of sound, color and movement. Here, lastly, is the constructive imagination that makes each separate poem play its part in a larger plan. As for the place of "The River" in this plan, I think I have shown that it succeeds in the two functions it was called upon to perform. At the same time, considered apart from the volume as a whole, it has a life of its own; and it has a separate structure also, one which might be compared to that of an ideal Chrysler Building. Just as the building stands broadly in a rubble of houses, narrows to a tower, rises implacably story after story, and finally soars upward in one clean shaft; so the poem, which began as a crazy jumble of prose and progressed by narrowing circles into the Great Valley, develops finally into a slow hymn to the river, a celebration of the Mississippi as it pours "down two more turns—"

> *And flows within itself, heaps itself free.*
> *All fades but one thin skyline 'round. . . . Ahead*
> *No embrace opens but the stinging sea;*
> *The River lifts itself from its long bed,*

Poised wholly on its dream, a mustard glow
Tortured with history, its one will—flow!
—The Passion spreads in wide tongues, choked and slow,
Meeting the Gulf, hosannas silently below.

Louis Untermeyer

Prophetic Rhapsody

The poetry of Hart Crane is, for all its *finesse* of delineation, founded on rhetoric, but rhetoric of a new order. His earlier work established his relation to Rimbaud, Poe, and Wallace Stevens— poets devoted to tonal nuances, tangential allusions, and verbal color—Crane's effects being often as ingenious and accomplished as theirs. Frequently he transcended ingenuity, striking out phrases of sudden clarity. But "White Buildings" was the record of esthetic as well as emotional conflicts. Alternating between clipped characterization and complete departure from representation, the lines approximated without quite achieving an "absolute" poetry. As Allen Tate hinted in his introduction to Crane's first volume, the poet had not yet discovered a theme to embody his uncoördinated visions.

In "The Bridge" the theme has been found. A set of disparate poems has been integrated by vital figures, the figures having been lifted into the realm of national myth. The sense of time flows like a leading theme through variations, interruptions, dissonances, and disruptions until a pattern emerges. In that pattern,

From *The Saturday Review of Literature.* VI (June 14, 1930), 1125. Reprinted by permission of *Saturday Review.*

sometimes obscure but finally resolved, Pocahontas and Paumanok, Rip Van Winkle and the Wright Brothers, Atlantic and the Brooklyn Bridge are not isolated phenomena but are significantly related, and—even in their most realistic aspects—take on legendary proportions.

> Stars scribble on our eyes the frosty sagas,
> The gleaming cantos of unvanquished space . . .
> O sinewy silver biplane, nudging the wind's withers!
> There, from Kill Devils Hill at Kitty Hawk
> Two brothers in their twinship left the dune;
> Warping the gale, the Wright windwrestlers veered
> Capeward, then blading the wind's flank, banked and spun
> What ciphers risen from prophetic script,
> What marathons new-set between the stars!
> The soul, by naphtha fledged into new reaches
> Already knows the closer clasp of Mars,—
> New latitudes, unknotting, soon give place
> To what fierce schedules, rife of doom apace!
>
> Behold the dragon's covey—amphibian, ubiquitous
> To hedge the seaboard, wrap the headland, ride
> The blue's unfeathered districts unto aether . . .
> While Iliads glimmer through eyes raised in pride
> Hell's belt springs wider—into heaven's plumed side.

Such a fragment, torn from the section "Cape Hatteras" (which appeared originally in the columns of this weekly) conveys a small —a very small—sense of the synthesis which molds the separate parts of "The Bridge" into an organized whole. The influences have not been wholly discarded: one does not have to look far to recognize the color-suggestiveness of Stevens and the contrast-method of Pound and Eliot. Yet it is equally evident that Crane is not spiritually persuaded by any of these, but by poets who might be thought their opposites. His visions—his very mottoes—are those of Blake, the Book of Job, Emily Dickinson, Walt Whitman. It is the spirit of Whitman—the spirit of "competent loam, the probable grass"—which is apotheosized on a rising cadence; from the "red, eternal flesh of Pocohontas" to the taut motors "space-gnawing" past auroral beaches, the younger poet pursues the cosmic Lounger of the Open Road.

As a sheer phrase-maker Crane commands attention. His work is studded with images and epithets like "Where the cedar leaf divides the sky," "the nasal whine of power whips a new universe," "thunder's eloquence through green arcades," "thewed of the levin, thunder-shod and lean," "the agile precincts of the lark's return."

Yet it is not phrase-making that chiefly distinguishes Crane; it is the apostrophic power, the strangely tuned but undeniable eloquence which makes "The Bridge" an important contribution to recent American poetry. Here is the accepted distortion and telescoping of time-space which has become, it seems, part of every modernist's equipment; here is the mechanism of "The Waste Land" and the Poundian "Cantos" giving shape to scattered symphonic passages. But here also is a passion that mounts to a sometimes broken but finally sustained rhapsody. "The Bridge" is manifestly prophetic.

There will be those who will still find Crane's poetry not only tangential but cryptic, and it must be admitted that his combination of allusiveness and allegory is a handicap to "the plain reader" since the allusions are often remote and the allegorical symbols personal to the point of privacy. But whatever Crane loses in directness he gains in a realism beyond factual reality; instead of the expected sharp-edged statement he has perfected a rounded locution from which the meaning is always on the point of sliding off and yet maintaining something more than the surface meaning. It is a triumph of suggestion, an exact inexactitude in which the implications are more important than the half-evaded fact. But it is not so much the employment of his symbols as their movement which makes the scheme of the new book so much larger than the program of "White Buildings." "The Bridge" carries the rhetorician beyond himself. Its intention is inclusive, even grandiose; its reach is lofty; its achievement indubitable. It approaches—if such a thing is possible—a highly sophisticated, highly syncopated local epic.

William Rose Benét

Round about Parnassus

Since the appearance of Robinson Jeffers none of the more recent male American poets has received greater encomia than has Hart Crane. And this arose immediately with the publication of his "White Buildings." We ourself derived very little from "White Buildings" save the impression of a wild talent which might make itself articulate when it chose to submit to some of the means of communication afforded by a proper use of the English language, which has proved quite flexible enough for greater writers who chose to use and not abuse its syntax. Undoubtedly a gift for imagery appeared in this newcomer, undoubtedly an intensity of feeling and a sensitivity to mood. And there was always the reckless reach for striking phrase which more than half the time eluded the grasp. Rhetoric there was in abundance, and rhetoric there is in abundance in Mr. Crane's latest, and second, volume, "The Bridge," which is the most ambitious flight he has yet attempted. It endeavors to wrest from its breast the full significance of Northern America, the utilitarian grace and beauty of the Brooklyn

From *The Saturday Review of Literature,* VI (July 5, 1930), 1176. Reprinted by permission of *Saturday Review.*

13

Bridge—such grace and beauty as always abides in great engineering—being its myth and symbol.

Dispensing with the book's dust cover, loaded with quotations
from the poet's admirers, we gave ourselves to the poem itself, the
mere binding of which is dignified and striking. We read the poem
through at a sitting, no great feat, inasmuch as it is not very long.
The total impression made is that the author is an outstanding
modern writer. He has, perhaps, a touch—how slight or great it
may be we are not prepared to say—of the thing called genius.
He has the fire in his bowels. And he does things to the English
language that make us wish to scream in torment.

The use of intransitive verbs as transitive verbs, the use of
nouns as verbs, the jarring of mismated adjectives and nouns, the
typographical tricks, so many wild phrases like "Who grindest oar,
and arguing the mast Subscribest holocaust of ships," a great deal
of sound and fury in reality signifying very little, cannot negate
the fact that on occasion the cascading fervor of this poet's speech
sweeps aside his obvious faults and raises the rainbow of his vision
before our eyes. Nor may one scientifically analyze the spectrum
of that rainbow, except to say that, in spite of his homage to
Whitman, it seems to be his own. He has borrowed technical devices here and there, and has not thoroughly assimilated them.
He is, once more, but half articulate. He has failed in creating
what might have been a truly great poem, failed through the im-
patience and overconcern with mere impressionism which are characteristics of this age. One feels that though he has observed
keenly and sometimes minutely the life about him, though he has
read history with intuition, and though he has grasped swiftly
some of the potencies of the tongue he speaks, he has need of a
mental discipline that would teach him organization and control
of his material.

One hesitates to say this of a young poet, because one of the
virtues of the early work of a man who has not yet quite come into
his own lies often in blazing his own trail and learning from the
mistakes of his ambitions. And some of Mr. Crane's most successful moments are due to his sheer recklessness; he is an unbaffled
though not always a successful Prometheus. Or he is like the
bloody sparrow that climbed up the bloody spout. His farewell to
the Bridge in the last section of his poem, "Atlantis," soars
through such verbiage indeed that he eventually declares:

> *Migrations that must needs void memory,*
> *Inventions that cobblestone the heart,—*

> *Unspeakable Thou Bridge to Thee, O Love.*
> *Thy pardon for this history, whitest Flower,*
> *O Answerer of all,—Anemone,—*
> *Now while thy petals spend the suns about*
> *us, hold—*
> *(O Thou whose radiance doth inherit me)*
> *Atlantis,—hold thy floating singer late!*

which is indeed rather hard to disentangle. It is, at best, but a fervent stammer.

But to realize the force of this poem one must not read it piecemeal. One must make the best of certain apparently undecipherable passages. Mr. Crane can invoke the Bridge in much more inspired terms, as in his Proem:

> *And Thee, across the harbor, silver-paced*
> *As though the sun took step of thee, yet left*
> *Some motion ever unspent in thy stride,—*
> *Implicitly thy freedom staying thee!*

After the Proem we hear Columbus speaking in "Ave Maria" where

> *. . . waves climb into dusk on gleaming*
> *mail;*
> *Invisible valves of the sea,—locks, tendons*
> *Crested and creeping, troughing corridors*
> *That fall back yawning to another plunge.*

He is to bring back Cathay, as he believes. Section II, "Powhatan's Daughter," begins with "Harbor Dawn," almost wholly successful, and follows with "Van Winkle," "The River" (perhaps the most powerful division of this section), and "The Dance," in which the spirit of Pocahontas first truly appears.

> *We danced, O Brave, we danced beyond their*
> *farms,*
> *In cobalt desert closures made our vows. . . .*
> *Now is the strong prayer folded in thine*
> *arms,*
> *The serpent with the eagle in the boughs.*

This is followed by "Indiana," a pioneer mother's farewell to her son, a sentimental interlude, to which succeed "Cutty Sark," "Cape Hatteras," and "Three Songs." We cannot but think that

Mr. Crane is at his best when he deals with the sea, save for the remarkable section following on "Three Songs" and "Quaker Hill," successive as they are to "Cape Hatteras." The section to which we refer is entitled "The Tunnel," and we know of no poem about a ride on the Interborough under the river which could better it. "The Tunnel" comes directly before the final section, "Atlantis." It might be said to furnish an Inferno to be contrasted with a Paradiso. When "The Bridge" is concluded we have had glimpses of a great deal of America. We have been reminded of the special American significance Vachel Lindsay found in the legend of Pocahontas, we have recalled Herman Melville, "Cape Hatteras" has yielded up Walt Whitman, we have looked on the gigantic Mississippi, and the ghost of Edgar Allan Poe has ridden with us on the subway. We have adventured with the airplanes of this modern age. We have had variety enow.

And, to speak for ourself, we found it all quite fascinating. Our demurrer is entered against too great haphazardness in the organization of the material and against phraseology that often clots against all sense and that even sometimes descends to the banal. But there is a sweep to this poem; it is a most interesting failure; and it reveals potencies in the author that may make his next work even more remarkable.

Yvor Winters

The Progress of Hart Crane

It is necessary, before attempting to criticize Mr. Crane's new book, to place it in the proper genre and to give as accurate an account as one is able of its theme. The book cannot be called an epic, in spite of its endeavor to create and embody a national myth, because it has no narrative framework and so lacks the formal unity of an epic. It is not didactic, because there is no logical exposition of ideas; neither Homer nor Dante will supply a standard of comparison. The structure we shall find is lyrical; but the poem is not a single lyric, it is rather a collection of lyrics on themes more or less related and loosely following out of each other. The model, in so far as there is one, is obviously Whitman, whom the author proclaims in this book as his master.

The book is composed of eight parts, of which two contain more than one lyric. There is a *Proem: To Brooklyn Bridge*, in which the initial inspiration of the book is suggested. Part I, *Ave Maria*, is a monologue spoken by Columbus on his first return to Spain; one receives the impression that Columbus is not only the herald

From *Poetry*, XXXVI (June 1930), 153-65. Copyright 1930 by The Modern Poetry Association. Reprinted by permission of the Editor of *Poetry* and Janet Lewis Winters, executrix of the estate of Yvor Winters.

of the new world to the old, but that he is in some way the herald of life to the unborn. Part II, *Powhatan's Daughter*, deals with the soil, the flesh of the continent (Pocahontas), and is composed of five lyrics: the first, *Harbor Dawn*, shows a protagonist, perhaps the author, or better simply man, awakening not only to day but to life after "400 years and more . . . or is it from the soundless shore of sleep?"; the second, *Van Winkle*, give a kind of fragmentary glimpse of American boyhood (the boy is Van Winkle, one gathers, because he is exploring the new world in a somewhat dazed condition after "400 years and more"); the third, *The River*, shows the adolescent joining the vagrants and coming to his first realization of the soil, the body of Pocahontas; the fourth, *The Dance*, projects the personality of the author into an imagined Indian brave, Maquokeeta, whose apotheosis at the stake and amid a war dance effects a permanent and spiritual union with Pocahontas; fifth, *Indiana*, depicts an old pioneer bidding goodbye to her adopted son, who is setting out in search of adventure. Part III, *Cutty Sark*, is a kind of ghost-dance of the old clippers, the early days of American navigation. Part IV, *Cape Hatteras*, is a long prayer to Walt Whitman, into the midst of which is inserted a brief history of aviation, beginning with the first flight of the Wrights and ending with a contemporary crash; the exact relationship of this section to the book as a whole remains obscure to me, as does the formal intention of the lyric itself. Part V is composed of *Three Songs*, which provide an interlude and which deal in a purer and more condensed form with themes treated elsewhere. The intention of the sixth section, *Quaker Hill*, remains as obscure to me as that of the fourth; the poem is prefaced by selections from Isadora Duncan and Emily Dickinson, both of whom are mentioned in the poem as symbols, one would guess, of the Quaker, Puritan, and other "ideals" of the past, the decay of which the poem indicates; these constituting a combination that is almost enough to freeze the blood of one with my own prejudices and inhibitions. Part VII, *The Tunnel*, deals with the subway, the modern metropolitan Purgatory, the trial and purification by fire and hallucination, in which the ghost of Poe appears to be rather incidentally entangled. Part VIII, *Atlantis*, is the apotheosis of the bridge addressed in the proem, in the form of the new Atlantis, the future America. It ends with Mr. Crane's version of Whitman's "Look for me under your bootsoles":

O Answerer of All,—Anemone,—
Now while thy petals spend the suns about us, hold—

(O Thou whose radiance doth inherit me)
Atlantis,—hold thy floating singer late!

I do not offer this analysis as complete or final, but as the best
I have been able to devise so far; I have discovered in the past
that Mr. Crane's work is likely to clear up in a measure with
familiarity. Nevertheless, it should be apparent from the looseness
of the progression—and it will be more apparent after an inspection of the variety of meters—that the book as a whole has no
more unity than the *Song of Myself;* it must be treated, as I have
said, as a series of lyrics on a theme that is basically Whitmanian,
but that, under the influence of Blake and Mr. Crane's own inclinations, is extended into regions with which Whitman did not
concern himself.

Now Whitman doubtless regarded himself as something of an
epic writer, and it is possible that Mr. Crane feels that he is one;
the difference between Whitman (who is his own epic hero) and
pius Aeneas is that the latter is not only obeying destiny, he is
obeying his mother. That is, destiny, for Aeneas, is not a vague
surge toward an infinite future, it is a deliberate effort to achieve
a definite aim, and the effort is composed of specific moral duties;
it is the serious attitude toward those duties that made him *pius*
to the Augustan Roman. It is the same attitude that gives to
every one of his acts a definite and absolutely individual value, as
well as a definite bearing on the theme of the book as a whole.
That is, destiny for Vergil was a clear and comprehensible thing
and had a clear relationship to a complete scale of human values.
Whitman found all human values about equal and could envisage
good only as an enthusiastic acceptance of everything at hand;
but if nothing is bad it follows equally that nothing is good—that
is, everything is equivalent to everything else and there are no
values at all; unless one can envisage as good a kind of meaningless and inexhaustible energy, or unless one can face about with
Mr. Jeffers and regard annihilation, complete negation, as the only
good. It is therefore natural that Whitman's poems, like Mr.
Jeffers' should be little save boundless catalogues. Both of these
poets, and Mr. Crane as well, are headed precisely for nowhere,
in spite of all the shouting. All three are occasionally betrayed by
their talents into producing a passage better than their usual run,
but this only goes to prove the fallacy of their initial assumptions.
Mr. Crane, since he possesses the greatest genius in the Whitmanian tradition, and since, strangely enough, he grafts onto the
Whitmanian tradition something of the stylistic discipline of the

Symbolists, most often exceeds himself in this manner. The Whitmanian basis of Mr. Crane's book makes a hero, as I have said, impossible. And the "destiny" of a nation is hard to get at in the abstract, since it is a vague generality, like "the French temperament" or "the average American." It reduces itself, when one comes to describe it—without a hero—to the most elementary and the least interesting aspects of the general landscape, aspects which cannot possibly be imbued with any definite significance, no matter how excited one may get, for the simple reason that no definite significance is available. It is on this rock that *Atlantis* shatters; and on a similar rock, we shall presently see, occurs the wreck of *The Dance*, the other climax of the volume.

There is only one poem in the volume that endeavors to treat clearly of an individual human relationship; the poem is *Indiana*, and it fails miserably—it could scarcely be more mawkish and helpless. The fact is unimportant except that it strengthens one's suspicion that Mr. Crane is temperamentally unable to understand a very wide range of experience, and one's feeling that even his best poems—which, in spite of this limitation, are very fine— have about them something of the fragility of innocence. The two most powerful poems in the book, though they are not the most perfect, are *The River* and *The Dance*.

The River falls into three distinct and unsynthesized parts. The first is a catalogue of the "din and slogans of the year"—prefatory information thrown at one in the raw and absolutely unmastered. The second part, which deals with the hoboes, the intercessors with Pocahontas "who have touched her knowing her without name," is better organized but is still turgid and confused; it has magnificent moments. The third part—each of the three parts is metrically distinct from the rest—though not quite as clean as Mr. Crane's finest writing, carries the epic quality of the Whitmanian vision (the vision of humanity *en masse*, or undifferentiated) to the greatest dignity and power of which it is, probably, capable; the stream of humanity becomes fused, poetically, with the stream of the Mississippi, and the result is a passage of extraordinary poetry:

> Down, down—born pioneers in time's despite,
> Grimed tributaries to an ancient flow—
> They win no frontier by their wayward plight,
> But drift in stillness, as from Jordan's brow.
>
> You will not hear it as the sea; even stone
> Is not more hushed by gravity. . . . But slow,

As loth to take more tribute—sliding prone
Like one whose eyes were buried long ago

The River, spreading, flows—and spends your dream.
What are you, lost within this tideless spell?
You are your father's father, and the stream—
A liquid theme that floating niggers swell.

The complete passage contains eight stanzas of mounting intensity; it has a few faults of detail, but I cannot read it—much less
read it aloud—without being profoundly moved.

The Dance is more even, but chiefly because it is more evenly
impure. I have already indicated briefly the theme of *The Dance*.
It is in the following stanza that the apotheosis of Maquokeeta
begins:

O, like the lizard in the furious noon,
That drops his legs and colors in the sun,
—And laughs, pure serpent, Time itself, and moon
Of his own fate, I saw thy change begun!

It is obvious from such a stanza that we are analyzing the flaws
in a genius of a high order—none of the famous purple patches in
Shelley, for example, surpasses this stanza, and probably none
equals it; so be it. But the flaws in Mr. Crane's genius are, I
believe, so great as to partake, if they persist, almost of the nature
of a public catastrophe. The most that we can learn about the
nature of the apotheosis follows a few lines further on:

Thy freedom is her largesse, Prince, and hid
On paths thou knewest best to claim her by.

High unto Labrador the sun strikes free
Her speechless dream of snow, and stirred again,
She is the torrent and the singing tree;
And she is virgin to the last of men. . . .

And when the caribou slant down for salt
Do arrows thirst and leap? Do antlers shine
Alert, star-triggered in the listening vault
Of dusk?—And are her perfect brows to thine?

These lines are in themselves, for the most part, very good;
placed in the proper poetic setting and with an adequate ideational
background, they might contribute to a wholly sound poem. Here,
however, they represent the climax of that poem which would

appear to be intended as one of the two climactic points of the sequence. They constitute an assertion of the faith on which the sequence is built; there is no evidence here or elsewhere in the poem or the book that they are merely a poetic and incomplete hint of a more definite belief; and there is a great deal of evidence that Mr. Crane suspects continually the inadequacy of his belief, or at any rate is continually hampered and frustrated by that inadequacy. Mr. Crane demands of his medicine-man to "lie to us—dance us back the tribal morn." Let us examine another passage:

> Spears and assemblies: black drums thrusting on—
> O yelling battlements,—I, too, was liege
> To rainbows currying each pulsant bone:
> Surpassed the circumstance, danced out the siege!
>
> And buzzard-circleted, screamed from the stake;
> I could not pick the arrows from my side.
> Wrapped in that fire, I saw more escorts wake—
> Flickering, sprint up the hill groins like a tide.

Any one of these lines is a brilliant performance; but only two of them, I believe, at the most, are brilliant on a poetic level—the fourth (possibly) and the sixth. The sixth is worthy of Racine. The others are brilliant on what I should call a descriptive level. To make this clear, I offer several others taken nearly at random from the same poem:

> A cyclone threshes in the turbine crest,
> Swooping in eagle feathers down your back.
>
> I left my sleek boat nibbling margin grass.
>
> I learned to catch the trout's moon-whisper.

These lines, though they are perceived with great precision, have no evident connection with the theme except as they are a part of the natural landscape, and that connection is inadequate for art. One feels no fluid experience bathing the perceptions and giving them a significant relation; one feels rather fact after fact, each, or nearly each, admirably presented but only very casually relevant, being hurled at one by the author in a fine frenzy as if he were trying to convince one, to hypnotize one, that he might in turn be convinced himself.

There are moments throughout the poem when the hypnosis is achieved, and lines of pure electricity occur; but the lapse to the descriptive is sudden and immediate. The poem is composed mainly of unfused details, and is excited rather than rhythmic. The quality which we call restraint, and which is here lacking, is the result of a feeling on the part of a poet that the motivation of his emotion is sound and needs no justification, that the emotion is inevitable; his problem, then, is only to give order to his emotion. In Mr. Crane we see an attempt to emotionalize a theme to the point where both he and the reader will forget to question its justification. It is, whatever fragmentary success may result from it, a form of hysteria. In this case the author is endeavoring to evoke a plane of experience higher than that of this world, about which he knows nothing and is able to imagine little or nothing, by the use of details taken from the plane of experience (this world) from which he is trying to escape. The details, as I have said, are good, but they almost never have meaning, for the simple reason that the meaning is not available. I do not wish to imply that a wholly concrete statement may not have poetic value—it may, as in some of the best work of the Imagists and the Imagist fringe (Dr. Williams, Miss Moore, and so on), if the author is clearly aware of the value when he writes it; if, in other words, the feeling is definitely implicated in the perception. *Atlantis*, as I have already said, is an attempt to embody another non-existent "destiny" in miscellaneous concrete details. It contains, like *The Dance*, superb poetry; unlike *The Dance*, its low spots are imprecise—in place of exact description we get vague thunder.

The same faults of rhetoric are to be found in *National Winter Garden*, one of the *Three Songs*, but are almost absent from the first of its companion pieces, *Southern Cross*, a poem which very nearly, though not quite, equals the two most perfect poems, to my mind, that Mr. Crane has written, *Repose of Rivers* and *Voyages II*, from his former volume. *The Harbor Dawn*, *Van Winkle*, *The Tunnel*, *Cape Hatteras*, and *Quaker Hill* are too vague in detail and chaotic in form to be worth much; *Cape Hatteras*, indeed, in its attitude toward Whitman, strikes me as desperately sentimental. Mr. Crane's estimate of Whitman and his complete failure to understand Emily Dickinson (for which see his charming but uncomprehending poem addressed to her and published several years ago in *The Nation*) are of a piece not only with each other but with his own failures and limitations as a poet.

Cutty Sark is a frail but exquisite and almost incomparably skilful dance of shadows. Its conclusion is a perpetual delight. It is a kind of radio question sent into the past to locate certain lost clippers, clippers the names of which, though apparently made for Mr. Crane's purpose, are historical:

Buntlines tusseling (91 days, 20 hours and anchored!)
                                    Rainbow, Leander
(last trip a tragedy) where can you be
Nimbus? and you rivals two—
        a long tack keeping—

                                        Taeping?
                                        Ariel?

The remaining poems—the *Proem* and *Ave Maria*—are, so far as
I can see, basically sound; that is, I am aware of no earthly reason
why Mr. Crane should not write a poem expressing his admiration
of the Brooklyn Bridge, or an imaginary monologue spoken by
Columbus. Both poems contain fine things; both, unfortunately,
contain a great deal that is empty. As in *Atlantis*, the weak
portions are composed of inexact poetic verbiage. These poems
illustrate the danger inherent in Mr. Crane's almost blind faith in
his moment-to-moment inspiration, the danger that the author
may turn himself into a kind of stylistic automaton, the danger
that he may develop a sentimental leniency toward his vices and
become wholly their victim, instead of understanding them and
eliminating them.

Mr. Crane is not alone in this danger; it is one of the greatest
dangers of the entire body of anti-intellectualist literature of our
time. It can be seen in Miss Roberts' latest novel, *The Great
Meadow*, a book in which the dangers potential in the style of her
first two novels have become actual and almost smother a good
plot. It can be seen in a good deal of the latest work of Mr. Joyce,
who, while revolutionizing the word, spends an appalling lot of
detailed revolution telling us how little clouds commit suicide
and the like. It can be seen, I regret above all to add, in the last
three or four years' work of Dr. Williams, whose experiments in
perpetual motion are becoming so repetitious as to appear very
nearly mechanical or even static. Dr. Williams, though a writer of
greater range and mastery, in all likelihood, than any of these
others, is a bigot and is bound to be the victim of his own bigotry
just as are the intellectual bigots whom he damns. Mr. Frost, at
the age of fifty-odd, can continue to grow amazingly. Mr. Joyce
and Dr. Williams appear to be disintegrating in their forties, Miss
Roberts and Mr. Crane in their thirties. Thomas Hardy could
grow in his eighties. Two things would appear certain about the
situation: it is profoundly alarming, and it is not inevitable.

It is possible that Mr. Crane may recover himself. In any event,
he has given us, in his first book, several lyrics that one is tempted
to call great, and in both books several charming minor lyrics and

many magnificent fragments. And one thing he has demonstrated, the impossibility of getting anywhere with the Whitmanian inspiration. No writer of comparable ability has struggled with it before, and, with Mr. Crane's wreckage in view, it seems highly unlikely that any writer of comparable genius will struggle with it again.

Allen Tate

Hart Crane[1]

The career of Hart Crane will be written by future critics as a chapter in the neo-symbolist movement. An historical view of his poetry at this time would be misleading and incomplete. Like most poets of his age in America, Crane discovered Rimbaud through Eliot and the Imagists; it is certain that long before he had done any of his best work he had come to believe himself the spiritual heir of the French poet. He had an instinctive mastery of the fused metaphor of symbolism, but it is not likely that he ever knew more of the symbolist poets than he had got out of Pound's *Pavannes and Divisions.* Whether Crane's style is symbolistic, or should, in many instances, like the first six or seven stanzas of "The River," be called Elizabethan, is a question that need not concern us now.

Between *The Bridge* and "Une Saison d'Enfer" there is little essential affinity. Rimbaud achieved "disorder" out of implicit

From *Essays of Four Decades* (Chicago: Swallow Press, 1968), pp. 310-23. Copyright 1968 by The Swallow Press Inc.
[1] This essay is composed of two papers written several years apart, the one in 1932, a few months after Crane's death, the other in 1937 as a review of Philip Horton's *Hart Crane: The Life of an American Poet.*

order, after a deliberate cultivation of "derangement," but in our age the disintegration of our intellectual systems is accomplished. With Crane the disorder is original and fundamental. That is the special quality of his mind that belongs peculiarly to our own time. His aesthetic problem, however, was more general; it was the historic problem of romanticism.

Harold Hart Crane, one of the great masters of the romantic movement, was born in Garrettsville, Ohio, on July 21, 1899. His birthplace is a small town near Cleveland, in the old Western Reserve, a region which, as distinguished from the lower portions of the state, where people from the Southern up-country settled, was populated largely by New England stock. He seems to have known little of his ancestry, but he frequently said that his maternal forebears had given Hartford, Connecticut, its name, and that they went "back to Stratford-on-Avon"—a fiction surely, but one that gave him distinct pleasure. His formal education was slight. After the third year at high school, when he was fifteen, it ended, and he worked in his father's candy factory in Cleveland, where the family had removed in his childhood. He repeatedly told me that money had been set aside for his education at college, but that it had been used for other purposes. With the instinct of genius he read the great poets, but he never acquired an objective mastery of any literature, or even of the history of his country—a defect of considerable interest in a poet whose most ambitious work is an American epic.

In any ordinary sense Crane was not an educated man; in many respects he was an ignorant man. There is already a Crane legend, like the Poe legend—it should be fostered because it will help to make his poetry generally known—and the scholars will decide it was a pity that so great a talent lacked early advantages. It is probable that he was incapable of the formal discipline of a classical education, and probable, too, that the eclectic education of his time would have scattered and killed his talent. His poetry not only has defects of the surface, it has a defect of vision; but its great and peculiar value cannot be separated from its limitations. Its qualities are bound up with a special focus of the intellect and sensibility, and it would be folly to wish that his mind had been better trained or differently organized.

The story of his suicide is well-known. The information that I have seems authentic, but it is incomplete and subject to excessive interpretation. Toward the end of April, 1932, he embarked on the S.S. *Orizaba* bound from Vera Cruz to New York. On the night of April 26 he got into a brawl with some sailors; he was

severely beaten and robbed. At noon the next day, the ship being
in the Caribbean a few hours out of Havana, he rushed from his
stateroom clad in pajamas and overcoat, walked through the smoking room out onto the deck, and then the length of the ship to
the stern. There without hesitation he made a perfect dive into
the sea. It is said that a life preserver was thrown to him; he
either did not see it or did not want it. By the time the ship had
turned back he had disappeared. Whether he forced himself down
—for a moment he was seen swimming—or was seized by a shark,
as the captain believed, cannot be known. After a search of thirty-
five minutes his body was not found, and the *Orizaba* put back
into her course.

In the summer of 1930 he had written to me that he feared his
most ambitious work, *The Bridge*, was not quite perfectly "realized," that probably his soundest work was in the shorter pieces
of *White Buildings*, but that his mind, being once committed to
the larger undertaking, could never return to the lyrical and more
limited form. He had an extraordinary insight into the foundations
of his work, and I think this judgment of it will not be refuted.

From 1922 to 1928—after that year I saw him and heard from
him irregularly until his death—I could observe the development
of his style from poem to poem; and his letters—written always in
a pure and lucid prose—provide a valuable commentary on his
career. This is not the place to bring all this material together for
judgment. As I look back upon his work and its relation to the
life he lived, a general statement about it comes to my mind that
may throw some light on the dissatisfaction that he felt with his
career. It will be a judgment upon the life and works of a man
whom I knew affectionately for ten years as a friend.

Suicide was the sole act of will left to him short of a profound
alteration of his character. I think the evidence of this is the
locked-in sensibility, the insulated egoism, of his poetry—a subject that I shall return to. The background of his death was
dramatically perfect: a large portion of his finest imagery was of
the sea, chiefly the Caribbean:

> O minstrel galleons of Carib fire,
> Bequeath us to no earthly shore until
> Is answered in the vortex of our grave
> The seal's wide spindrift gaze toward paradise.

His verse is full of splendid images of this order, a rich symbolism
for an implicit pantheism that, whatever may be its intrinsic merit,
he had the courage to vindicate with death in the end.

His pantheism was not passive and contemplative; it rose out of the collision between his own locked-in sensibility and the ordinary forms of experience. Every poem is a thrust of that sensibility into the world: his defect lay in his inability to face out the moral criticism implied in the failure to impose his will upon experience.

The Bridge is presumably an epic. How early he had conceived the idea of the poem and the leading symbolism, it is difficult to know; certainly as early as February, 1923. Up to that time, with the exception of "For the Marriage of Faustus and Helen" (1922), he had written only short poems, but most of them, "Praise for an Urn," "Black Tambourine," "Paraphrase," and "Emblems of Conduct,"[2] are among his finest work. It is a mistake then to suppose that all of *White Buildings* is early experimental writing; a large portion of that volume, and perhaps the least successful part of it, is made up of poems written after *The Bridge* was begun. "Praise for an Urn" was written in the spring of 1922—one of the finest elegies by an American poet—and although his later development gave us a poetry that the period would be much the less rich for not having, he never again had such perfect mastery of his subject—because he never again quite knew what his subject was.

Readers familiar with "For the Marriage of Faustus and Helen" admire it by passages, but the form of the poem, in its framework of symbol, is an abstraction empty of any knowable experience. The originality of the poem is in its rhythms, but it has the conventional diction that a young poet picks up in his first reading. Crane, I believe, felt that this was so; and he became so dissatisfied, not only with the style of the poem, which is heavily influenced by Eliot and Laforgue, but with the "literary" character of the symbolism, that he set about the greater task of writing *The Bridge*. He had looked upon his "Faustus and Helen" as an answer to the pessimism of the school of Eliot, and *The Bridge* was to be an even more complete answer.

There was a fundamental mistake in Crane's diagnosis of Eliot's problem. Eliot's "pessimism" grows out of an awareness of the decay of the individual consciousness and its fixed relations to the world; but Crane thought that it was due to something like pure "orneriness," an unwillingness "to share with us the breath released," the breath being a new kind of freedom that he identi-

---

[2] It is now known that this poem is an elaboration of a "sonnet" entitled "Conduct" by Samuel Greenberg. See *Poems* by Samuel Greenberg, edited by Harold Holden and Jack McManis (New York, 1947).

fied emotionally with the age of the machine. This vagueness of purpose, in spite of the apparently concrete character of the Brooklyn Bridge, which became the symbol of his epic, he never succeeded in correcting. The "bridge" stands for no well-defined experience; it differs from the Helen and Faust symbols only in its unliterary origin. I think Crane was deceived by this difference, and by the fact that Brooklyn Bridge is "modern" and a fine piece of "mechanics." His more ambitious later project permitted him no greater mastery of formal structure than the more literary symbolism of his youth.

The fifteen parts of *The Bridge* taken as one poem suffer from the lack of a coherent structure, whether symbolic or narrative: the coherence of the work consists in the personal quality of the writing—in mood, feeling, and tone. In the best passages Crane has perfect mastery over the quality of his style; but the style lacks an objective pattern of ideas elaborate enough to carry it through an epic or heroic work. The single symbolic image, in which the whole poem centers, is at one moment the actual Brooklyn Bridge; at another, it is any bridge or "connection"; at still another, it is a philosophical pun and becomes the basis of a series of analogies.

In "Cape Hatteras," the airplane and Walt Whitman are analogous "bridges" to some transcendental truth. Because the idea is variously metaphor, symbol, and analogy, it tends to make the poem static. The poet takes it up, only to be forced to put it down again *when the poetic image of the moment is exhausted.* The idea does not, in short, fill the poet's mind; it is the starting point for a series of short flights, or inventions connected only in analogy— which explains the merely personal passages, which are obscure, and the lapses into sentimentality. For poetic sentimentality is emotion undisciplined by the structure of events or ideas of which it is ostensibly a part. The idea is not objective and articulate in itself; it lags after the poet's vision; it appears and disappears; and in the intervals Crane improvises, often beautifully, as in the flight of the airplane, sometimes badly, as in the passage on Whitman in the same poem.

In the great epic and philosophical works of the past, notably *The Divine Comedy,* the intellectual groundwork is not only simple philosophically; we not only know that the subject is personal salvation, just as we know that Crane's is the greatness of America: we are given also the complete articulation of the idea down to the slightest detail, and we are given it objectively apart from anything that the poet is going to say about it. When the poet extends his perception, there is a further extension of the groundwork ready to meet it and discipline it, and to compel the sensibility of the poet to stick to the subject. It is a game of chess; neither side can move without consulting the other. Crane's difficulty is that of modern poets generally: they play the game with half of the men, the men of sensibility, and because sensibility can make any move, the significance of all moves is obscure.

If we subtract from Crane's idea its periphery of sensation, we have left only the dead abstraction, the Greatness of America, which is capable of elucidation neither on the logical plane nor in terms of a generally known idea of America.

The theme of *The Bridge* is, in fact, an emotional oversimplification of a subject matter that Crane did not, on the plane of narrative and idea, simplify at all. The poem is emotionally homogeneous and simple—it contains a single purpose; but because it is not structurally clarified it is emotionally confused. America stands for a passage into new truths. Is this the meaning of American history? The poet has every right to answer yes, and this he has done. But just what in America or about America stands for this? Which American history? The historical plot of the poem, which is the groundwork on which the symbolic bridge stands, is arbitrary and broken, where the poet would have gained an overwhelming advantage by choosing a single period or episode, a concrete event with all its dramatic causes, and by following it up minutely, and being bound to it. In short, he would have gained an advantage could he have found a subject to stick to.

Does American culture afford such a subject? It probably does not. After the seventeenth century the sophisticated history of the scholars came into fashion; our popular, legendary chronicles come down only from the remoter European past. It was a sound impulse on Crane's part to look for an American myth, some simple version of our past that lies near the center of the American consciousness; an heroic tale with just enough symbolism to give his mind both direction and play. The soundness of his purpose is witnessed also by the kind of history in the poem: it is inaccurate, and it will not at all satisfy the sticklers for historical fact. It is the history of the motion picture, of naïve patriotism. This is sound; for it ignores the scientific ideal of historical truth-in-itself, and looks for a cultural truth which might win the spontaneous allegiance of the people. It is on such simple integers

of truth, not truth of fact but of religious necessity, that men
unite. The American mind was formed by the eighteenth-century
Enlightenment, which broke down the European "truths" and
gave us a temper deeply hostile to the making of new religious
truths of our own.

The impulse in *The Bridge* is religious, but the soundness of
an impulse is no warrant that it will create a sound art form. The
form depends on too many factors beyond the control of the poet.
The age is scientific and pseudo-scientific, and our philosophy is
Dewey's instrumentalism. And it is possibly this circumstance
that has driven the religious attitude into a corner where it lacks
the right instruments for its defense and growth, and where it is
in a vast muddle about just what these instruments are. Perhaps
this disunity of the intellect is responsible for Crane's unphilo-
sophical belief that the poet, unaided and isolated from the people,
can create a myth.

If anthropology has helped to destroy the credibility of myths,
it has shown us how they rise: their growth is mysterious from
the people as a whole. It is probable that no one man ever put
myth into history. It is still a nice problem among higher critics,
whether the authors of the Gospels were deliberate myth-makers,
or whether their minds were simply constructed that way; but the
evidence favors the latter. Crane was a myth-maker, and in an age
favorable to myths he would have written a mythical poem in the
act of writing an historical one.

It is difficult to agree with those critics who find his epic a
single poem and as such an artistic success. It is a collection of
lyrics, the best of which are not surpassed by anything in American literature. The writing is most distinguished when Crane is
least philosophical, *when he writes from sensation.* "The River"
has some blemishes towards the end, but by and large it is a
masterpiece of order and style; it alone is enough to place Crane
in the first rank of American poets, living or dead. Equally good
but less ambitious are the "Proem: To Brooklyn Bridge," and
"Harbor Dawn," and "The Dance" from the section called "Powhatan's Daughter."

These poems bear only the loosest relation to the symbolic
demands of the theme; they contain allusions to the historical pattern or extend the slender structure of analogy running through
the poem. They are primarily lyrical, and each has its complete
form. The poem "Indiana," written presumably to complete the
pattern of "Powhatan's Daughter," does not stand alone, and it is

one of the most astonishing failures ever made by a poet of Crane's genius. "The Dance" gives us the American background for the coming white man, and "Indiana" carries the stream of history to the pioneer West. It is a nightmare of sentimentality. Crane is at his most "philosophical" in a theme in which he feels no poetic interest whatever.

The structural defect of *The Bridge* is due to this fundamental contradiction of purpose. In one of his best earlier poems, "The Wine Menagerie," he exclaims: "New thresholds, new anatomies!" —new sensation, but he could not subdue the new sensation to a symbolic form.

His pantheism is necessarily a philosophy of sensation without point of view. An epic is a judgment of human action, an implied evaluation of a civilization, a way of life. In *The Bridge* the civilization that contains the subway hell of the section called "The Tunnel" is the same civilization of the airplane that the poet apostrophizes in "Cape Hatteras." There is no reason why the subway should be a fitter symbol of damnation than the airplane: both were produced by the same mentality on the same moral plane. There is a concealed, meaningless analogy between, on the one hand, the height of the plane and the depth of the subway, and, on the other, "higher" and "lower" in the religious sense. At one moment Crane faces his predicament of blindness to any rational order of value, and knows that he is damned; but he cannot face it long, and he tries to rest secure upon the intensity of sensation.

To the vision of the abyss in "The Tunnel," a vision that Dante passed through midway of this mortal life, Crane had no alternative: when it became too harrowing he cried to his Pocahontas, a typically romantic and sentimental symbol:

> Lie to us,—dance us back the tribal morn!

It is probably the perfect word of romanticism in this century. When Crane saw that his leading symbol, the bridge, would not hold all the material of his poem, he could not sustain it ironically, in the classical manner, by probing its defects; nor in the personal sections, like "Quaker Hill," does he include himself in his Leopardian denunciation of life. He is the blameless victim of a world whose impurity violates the moment of intensity, which would otherwise be enduring and perfect. He is betrayed, not by a defect of his own nature, but by the external world; he asks of nature, perfection—requiring only of himself, intensity. The persistent, and persistently defeated, pursuit of a natural absolute places Crane at the center of his age.

Alternately he asserts the symbol of the bridge and abandons it, because fundamentally he does not understand it. The idea of bridgeship is an elaborate blur leaving the inner structure of the poem confused.

Yet some of the best poetry of our generation is in *The Bridge*. Its inner confusion is a phase of the inner cross-purposes of the time. Crane was one of those men whom every age seems to select as the spokesmen of its spiritual life; they give the age away. The accidental features of their lives, their place in life, their very heredity, seem to fit them for their role; even their vices contribute to their preparation. Crane's biographer will have to study the early influences that confirmed him in narcissism, and thus made him typical of the rootless spiritual life of our time. The character formed by those influences represents an immense concentration, and becomes almost a symbol, of American life in this age.

Crane's poetry has incalculable moral value: it reveals our defects in their extremity. I have said that he knew little of the history of his country. It was not merely a defect of education, but a defect, in the spiritual sense, of the modern mind. Crane lacked the sort of indispensable understanding of his country that a New England farmer has who has never been out of his township. *The Bridge* attempts to include all American life, but it covers the ground with seven-league boots and, like a sightseer, sees nothing. With reference to its leading symbol, it has no subject matter. The poem is the effort of a solipsistic sensibility to locate itself in the external world, to establish points of reference.

It seems to me that by testing out his capacity to construct a great objective piece of work, in which his definition of himself should have been articulated, he brought his work to an end. I think he knew that the structure of *The Bridge* was finally incoherent, and for that reason—as I have said—he could no longer believe even in his lyrical powers; he could not return to the early work and take it up where he had left off. Far from "refuting" Eliot, his whole career is a vindication of Eliot's major premise—that the integrity of the individual consciousness has broken down. Crane had, in his later work, no individual consciousness: the hard firm style of "Praise for an Urn," which is based upon a inviolability, begins to disappear when the poet goes out into the clear-cut perception of moral relations, and upon their ultimate world and finds that the simplicity of a child's world has no universal sanction. From then on, instead of the effort to define himself in the midst of almost overwhelming complications—a situation that might have produced a tragic poet—he falls back upon the intensity of consciousness, rather than the clarity, for his center of vision. And that is romanticism.

His world had no center, and the thrust into sensation is responsible for the fragmentary quality of his most ambitious work. This thrust took two directions—the blind assertion of the will, and the blind desire for self-destruction. The poet did not face his first problem, which is to define the limits of his personality and to objectify its moral implications in an appropriate symbolism. Crane could only assert a quality of will against the world, and at each successive failure of the will he turned upon himself. In the failure of understanding—and understanding, for Dante, was a way of love—the romantic modern poet of the age of science attempts to impose his will upon experience and to possess the world.

It is this impulse of the modern period that has given us the greatest romantic poetry: Crane instinctively continued the conception of the will that was the deliberate discovery of Rimbaud. A poetry of the will is a poetry of sensation, for the poet surrenders to his sensations of the object in his effort to identify himself with it, and to own it. Some of Crane's finest lyrics—those written in the period of *The Bridge*—carry the modern impulse as far as you will find it anywhere in the French romantics. "Lachrymae Christi" and "Passage," though on the surface made up of pure images without philosophical meaning of the explicit sort in *The Bridge*, are the lyrical equivalents of the epic: the same kind of sensibility is at work. The implicit grasp of his material that we find in "Praise for an Urn," the poet has exchanged for an external, random symbol of which there is no possibility of realization. *The Bridge* is an irrational symbol of the will, of conquest, of blind achievement in space; its obverse is "Passage," whose lack of external symbolism exhibits the poetry of the will on the plane of sensation; and this is the self-destructive return of the will upon itself.

Criticism may well set about isolating the principle upon which Crane's poetry is organized. Powerful verse overwhelms its admirers, and betrays them into more than technical imitation. That is one of the arguments of Platonism against literature; it is the immediate quality of an art rather than its whole significance that sets up schools and traditions. Crane not only ends the romantic era in his own person; he ends it logically and morally. Beyond Crane no future poet can go. (This does not mean that the romantic impulse may not rise and flourish again.) The finest passages in his work are single moments in the stream of sensation; beyond the moment he goes at his peril; for beyond it lies the discrepancy between the sensuous fact, the perception, and its organizing symbol—a discrepancy that plunges him into sentimentality and chaos. But the "bridge" is empty and static, it has no inherent content, and the poet's attribution to it of the qualities of his own moral predicament is arbitrary. That explains the fragmentary and often unintelligible framework of the poem. There was neither complete action nor ordered symbolism in terms of which the distinct moments of perception could be clarified.

This was partly the problem of Rimbaud. But Crane's problem was nearer to the problem of Keats, and *The Bridge* is a failure in the sense that "Hyperion" is a failure, and with comparable magnificence. Crane's problem, being farther removed from the epic tradition, was actually more difficult than Keats's, and his treatment of it was doubtless the most satisfactory possible in our time. Beyond the quest of pure sensation and its ordering symbolism lies the total destruction of art. By attempting an extreme solution of the romantic problem Crane proved that it cannot be solved.

Karl Shapiro

Study of *Cape Hatteras* by Hart Crane

Everything about Hart Crane points to the poet possessed, the man in the grip of the demon. Three of his poetic ancestors, Poe, Baudelaire and Rimbaud, belong to the deepest mines of the poetic psyche; the fourth, Walt Whitman, presented him with the false vision of life which eventually Crane was to employ for his own self-destruction. Crane's instinct was for the depths, but through circumstance and innocence this instinct was translated into the will to die. His early work takes place aboveground; he will pause long enough to be hypnotized by the shine of white buildings.

> As silent as a mirror is believed
> Realities plunge in silence by. . .
>
> I am not ready for repentance;

When finally he is ready for repentance (the descent into the depths?) it will be too late to save himself. He has been shown

From *Poets at Work*, ed. Charles D. Abbott (New York: Harcourt, Brace & World, 1948), pp. 111-18. Copyright 1948 by Harcourt Brace Jovanich, Inc. Reprinted by permission of the publisher.

a false mythology in a mirror, and plunging after it he will die. *Ce ne peut être que la fin du monde, en avançant,* is the menacing superscription at the beginning of his first book. Narcissus is willing to plunge into the mirror; at any rate, he has caught a vision of his destiny. But between the journey and the suicide lies the heart-breaking road of disenchantment. At last the myth falls apart before his eyes, and the disappointment is too great to live with.

By the time the poet has come to write the *Cape Hatteras* segment of his epic, he already knows the futility of the poem. It is not only the weakest link in *The Bridge;* its inspiration, a kind of hymn to Whitman, threatens to poison the whole work.

Friends of Crane encouraged the poet to work over this section of *The Bridge* after it had advanced as far as the version I am going to discuss. Between this version* and the final form there must have been other worksheets; there are even differences between the Paris edition and the first American edition. Crane's method of composition kept him at work on a poem as long as it was available for improvement.

The majority of changes are external minor alterations made in the interest of a tighter meter or a more effective image.

> Imponderable the dinosaur who
> sinks slow,

in which the "who" is dropped. Or

> Or to recount the priests' march through Bombay—

becomes, without altering the number of syllables, a more exact description:

> Or how the priests walked—slowly through Bombay—

The internal changes, even in this advanced draft, are often of the greatest import. A comparison of the changes in the second stanza discloses a deepening of the image.

> To that deep wonderment, our native clay,
> Whose depth of red, eternal flesh of Pocahontas—
> Those continental folded aeons, surcharged

---

* The *Cape Hatteras* manuscript is not the property of the Lockwood Library, but is quoted here with the permission of its owner, Peter Blume.

With sweetness below derricks, chimneys, tunnels,
Is veined of that eternity that's pledged us . . .
While overhead, like corkscrew squeaks of radio static
The captured fume of space forms in the ears,
What whisperings of far lookouts on the main
Relapsing into silence . . . Time annuls—
Time, the serpent, retrieves the telescope,
Constricts it to its primal nest of vertigos,
The labyrinth, compressible, of our own egos.

Compare the final form.

To that deep wonderment, our native clay
Whose depth of red, eternal flesh of Pocahontus—
Those continental folded aeons, surcharged
With sweetness below derricks, chimneys, tunnels—
Is veined by all that time has really pledged us . . .
And from above, thin squeaks of radio static,
The captured fume of space foams in our ears—
What whisperings of far watches on the main
Relapsing into silence, while time clears
Our lenses, lifts a focus, resurrects
A periscope to glimpse what joys or pain
Our eyes can share or answer—then deflects
Us, shunting to a labyrinth submersed
Where each sees only his dim past reversed . . .

These turgid verses in the first form are trying, as it were, to end the poem. The serpent Time takes back the telescope, collapses it to the primal eye, the pool of our own egos. But this is too sudden for the poet, and he gives Time back the telescope while she clears the lenses and resurrects—a periscope. The meaning of this sleight-of-hand may lie in the "labyrinth submersed" which Crane presumably would like to reach. "The darkening pool" in the following stanza becomes "the lucid pool," a change, if changes mean anything at all, that is a rather desperate one. The fatal image of the mirror is again to the fore.

Left Hesperus mirrored in the lucid pool.

The poetry now becomes reckless, leaving the sea for the air, the submarine for the airplane.

Dream cancels dream in this new realm of fact
From which we wake into the dream of act;
Seeing himself an atom in a shroud—
Man hears himself an engine in a cloud!

"Hearing himself a locomotive in a cloud!" is the first attempt. The poet does not succeed in assimilating this machine imagery, as is his aim, but instead gives us a burlesque Blakian line. The succeeding stanza invokes Walt Whitman, and what is equally interesting, a sudden wraith, the spirit that portends the death of the watcher. The wraith does not appear except in the printed version. The poet asks Whitman if infinity

> Be still the same as when you walked the beach
> Near Paumanok—your lone patrol—and heard the wraith
> Through surf, its bird note there a long time falling . . .

The wraith might not be so prophetic after all, were it not for what follows. As in the tunnel, where Crane meets the demonic eyes of Poe—like agate lanterns—here the poet is pursued by the eyes of Whitman, which appear in the cliffs of Wall Street and "back over Connecticut pastures," but chiefly in the sea.

> Sea eyes and tidal, undenying, bright with myth!

It is as illuminating a line as the poet has written about himself and his apprehensions. It seems to rise from the same deeps as another poem about a drowned father which sings of "the pearls that were his eyes."

The following stanza is the well-known paean to machinery which begins "The nasal whine of power whips a new universe." It is not Crane at his best by any means, but it throws light on his curious method of composing, or rather bears out the connection of *artificial stimulation* and poetry in Crane's case. The poet's biographer records that Crane would sit at his desk with a jug of wine and a victrola going full blast, often repeating the same jazzy tune again and again.[1] Horton believes that the visionary fervor which Crane achieved by means of such stimuli could not have been awakened without some such agitation of the senses. Both music and liquor eventually became identified in Crane's mind with the process of composition. It is also recorded that the poet derived giddy and half-drunken sensations from machine noises, machine shapes, and the gigantic motions of machines. "Power's script,—wound, bobbin-bound, refined— / Is stropped to the slap of belts on booming spools, spurred / Into the bulging bouillon, harnessed jelly of the stars." This crude and unworked poetry

---

[1] Philip Horton, *Hart Crane, The Life of an American Poet.* Norton.

gives some idea of what he must have experienced before the
demon of the machine.

Following the machine passage there comes a long dizzying
adventure of the airplane. Two further images of sea-death disappear from the printed version of the poem. The draft reads:

> Two brothers in a twinship left the dune, the glazed lagoon,—

the final phrase being omitted from the book.

> Seductions blue and schedules rife of doom!

becomes

> To what fierce schedules, rife of doom apace!

The Wright brothers' theme leads into an excited vision of aerial
warfare. In some manner this battle is telescoped into the *Cape
Hatteras* theme, the purpose being to unify the poem as much as
possible. The draft version shows a large number of minor differences, and at least one of interest. The draft reads:

> O bright circumferences, heights employed to lift
> War's fiery kennel, interpolated red in vaporous offings:

which develops into

> O bright circumferences, heights employed to fly
> War's fiery kennel masked in downy offings,—

Nothing is gained, however. The poem is too far disrupted at this
stage to achieve unity.

Two stanzas down we come upon an unintelligible reference to
Sanskrit.

> Remember, Falcon-Eye,
> Thou hast a Sanscrit in thy sailor wrist, a charge
> To conjugate infinity's far verb anew . . . !

The printed version

> Remember, Falcon-Ace,
> Thou hast there in thy wrist a Sanskrit charge
> To conjugate infinity's dim marge—
> Anew . . . !

hardly clears up the puzzle, which might serve as reference to the inscrutability of the text as itself.

It will be useful to transcribe the original of the next passage that invokes Whitman, because it clarifies Crane's intent in the poem better than the finished version.

> But who has better held the heights than thou,
> O Walt?—Ascensions that bespeak in my own veins
> Thee at the junction elegiac, there, of speed
> With blank eternity. And thou dost wield the rebound seed.
> The inescapable equation there beyond, below
> The competent grass, the probable loam. O Walt,
> We wait, some of us, on the sand the ultimate frontier
> Not wings, but rhythm possible of wings!) . . .
> And thou shalt bide us there beyond our fall.
> For who was he but thou, who undertook the plunge,
> O carrier-creator of song's breakless chain!

The indigestible idea of Whitman as the carrier-creator who undertook the plunge drops from the revision, which in other respects also shows enormous improvement.

> The stars have grooved our eyes with old persuasions
> Of love and hatred, birth,—surcease of nations . . .
> But who has held the heights more sure than thou,
> O Walt!—Ascensions of thee hover in me now
> As thou at junctions elegiac, there, of speed
> With vast eternity, dost wield the rebound seed!
> The competent loam, the probable grass,—travail
> Of tides awash the pedestal of Everest, fail
> Not less than thou in pure impulse inbred
> To answer deepest soundings! O, upward from the dead
> Thou bringest tally, and a pact, new bound
> Of living brotherhood!

With more relevancy, Whitman is invoked as the spirit of the Mourner who has kept account of the wounds of armies from Appomattox to Somme. By now Crane has a binding thread of the tradition which he believes links him to Whitman, his Meistersinger. From here to the end of the poem there are virtually no changes of any kind, textual or otherwise. Either the poet has abandoned the poem or he feels that he has accomplished finality in the version. The ending of the poem is neither better nor worse than the rest of it: it is merely a little clearer.

Only so much can be said of the *Cape Hatteras* poem, in the draft and in the printed form. Unlike other sections of *The Bridge*, with the exception of the sentimental "Indiana," it is a piece of poorly conceived and poorly articulated work. That it foreshadows the poet's death is of course highly conjectural, but that it discusses some means and aspects of death in rapid sequence makes it possible for us to say that Crane at this time had already come face to face with his destiny. We do know that when the poet was writing *Cape Hatteras* he had lost the confidence of his vision; his personality was already disintegrating, but his talent proved itself at least once more in his last Mexican poem, *The Broken Tower*. The maudlin conclusion of *Cape Hatteras*, hand in hand with Walt, under a rainbow, is the defeated cry of a demonic poet who has lost his way. It is not the cry of a man who has lost his gift, which was the weak construction Crane chose to put upon his dilemma.

Brewster Ghiselin

Bridge into the Sea

In "The River," that part of *The Bridge* which is perhaps the major achievement of Hart Crane's poem, certain tramps are represented, men knowing intimately the earth's body—the earth of America: "Hobo-trekkers that forever search/An empire wilderness of freight and rails. . . . /—As I have trod the rumorous midnights, too." Possibly a part of Crane's interest in them came of his recognition of their resemblance, however obscure or slight, to himself. "Each seemed a child, like me. . . . Holding to childhood like some termless play." These men seem not to belong to the noonday. Almost fantasmal, they haunt the American place, ghostly survivors of the American story—for they are "pioneers in time's despite," but seekers who never find, since "They win no frontier." Without tangible position or solid accomplishment in the world, they exist a little apart, as if they had lost some connection with the whole American life the ideal development of which *The Bridge* purports to celebrate. They never ride the coaches that span the continent. They watch "the tail lights wizen and converge" or "jolted from the cold brake-beam" they die. With silt

From *Partisan Review,* XVI (July 1949), 679-86. © 1949 by *Partisan Review.* Reprinted by permission of the journal and the author.

and roots and "floating niggers" they are drawn down by the Mississippi, which drinks away the substance of the very continent, into the waters of the Gulf. With others, they "feed the River timelessly."

Despite their momentary prominence in the poem, they seem even less than unimportant. Crane refers to them as "Blind fists of nothing." And their disappearance seems inconsequential, a slight contribution amid all the tribute of earth to water. Yet what happens to them is of considerable import, as I hope to show.

There are other pioneers in the poem. Most significant is that first American pioneer, Columbus himself, whose exalted meditation as he approaches the shores of Spain form Part I of *The Bridge*. The voyage of Columbus, a journey yielding knowledge of a new world, is made to stand in *The Bridge* as type or pattern of a search undertaken by Crane's protagonist, a search for the full meaning of the master image of the poem, the symbolic Bridge. In pursuit of that essential knowledge, past and present are to be caught up into one integration and transmuted in an insight definitive of a worthy American destiny—a new world.

The Columbian voyage is a symbol well adapted to the expression of Crane's conscious intention, conquest of fresh meaning. The Bridge, the Span which by figurative extension unites the disparate parts of the physical continent and unifies the spiritual continent of men, is also a ship, means of passage and preservation amid the chaos of the waters. It is like that ship on whose ocean-spanning deck Columbus stands meditating "between two worlds," which are to be joined by his voyage:

> *For here between two worlds, another, harsh,*
> *This third, of water, tests the word. . . .*

Columbus found his new world, and by completing his voyage he opened the way to a new continent. Crane aspired to do likewise: penetrating into the unknown, to discover a new Cathay.

But he did not clearly see all that was involved in the way he had chosen. Or it is as if he had seen and could not face the truth, that the voyage which leads to his goal is a dark encounter with chaotic waters, a night passage, into disorder and doubt, the "eyes / Starved wide on blackened tides. . . ." That truth appears in the poem, but so veiled and distorted that it is impossible to believe that Crane understood his own expression of it. Again and again the protagonist is drawn to the water. But the black sea is too forbidding. Living, he will not dive into the sea. When as voyager he stands on a benighted deck, only twice and very briefly, in "Southern Cross" and "Atlantis," his eyes cling to the wake.

The encounter with dark waters, either in a night voyage or a dive into unknown depths, is a familiar symbol in psycho-analytical literature. It is often thought of as a bath of renewal, because it represents the first stage of an experience in which refreshment and readjustment are attained through subordinating to the psychic life as a whole the fixed, strictly determined, self-perpetuating elements of consciousness. The voyage or the dive symbolizes a surrender of consciousness in a search for the unconscious life. Some such yielding of the determinate to the indeterminate is a necessary step in all inner development, including that which takes place in invention, in the creative process. Whether in art or thought, a disordering, or a suspension of order, precedes the attainment of fresh insight. Crane's impulse toward the waters is thus understandable as essentially right and normal. It is part of his human need as a creative individual.

In his conscious intention, Crane did not commit his protagonist to the adventure into darkness. Yet the encounter with the chaos of the sea is the most compelling theme of *The Bridge*: not the consciously accepted theme of order established, but the theme of order destroyed. It elicits Crane's profoundest excitement and sustains his greatest poetry. That theme appears most clearly in "The River." The poem begins with images of "the cultural confusion of the present," as Crane himself declared. His own comment on his poem is instructive: "My tramps are psychological vehicles, also. Their wanderings, as you will notice, carry the reader into interior after interior, all of it funneled by the Mississippi. They are the left-overs of the pioneers in at least this respect—that abstractly their wanderings carry the reader through certain experiences roughly parallel to that of the traders, adventurers, Boone and others. I think I have caught some of the essential spirit of the Great Valley here, and in the process have approached the primal world of the Indian, which emerges with a full orchestra in the succeeding 'Dance.'" The tramps lead us across space and time, into legendary depths. It is a descent into the American origins of the poet's imagination. But it is something further, for it goes beyond the legend, goes into the waters of the funnelling Mississippi, which drags the continent and its creatures into the sea where all form and substance physical and psychical, the shapes of things and the memory of things, are dissolved:

The River, spreading, flows—and spends your dream.
What are you, lost within this tideless spell?
You are your father's father, and the stream—

Precisely that: lost in the racial stream, you are identified with
your ancestors in the course of a regression toward the depths of
the impersonal psychic life, the sea, which Crane represented as
the goal of the River.

This approach to dissolution is one of the most firmly established things in the poem. The Bridge leads in due course across
the land, in apparent affirmation of the integrity it purports to
symbolize. Yet in the very heart of the continent the land is
denied, dragged into the Gulf, deserted for the sea. The Bridge
becomes therefore a bridge into the waters of oblivion, a projection over which all of the established world might have been made
to walk the plank.

But the piracy did not succeed. The tramps, "pioneers in time's
despite," express the direction of Crane's own creative development, his orientation toward the deeps of the psyche. But Crane
did not grasp their significance and exploit it. The theme of
dissolution is not realized fully either here or elsewhere in *The
Bridge*. For, though Crane desired intensely to surrender himself
to the sea, it seemed to him that only the dead attain that goal.
The beloved Bridge, his ship, became a prison, because he would
not allow it to carry him into the darkness of the unlimited sea.

Crane's reluctance to indulge his impulse toward the water appears to have been determined not only by deathly fear but by an
excessive attachment to the established order. The explanation
may lie in the fact of his sexual inversion. In terms of jargon
currently used to describe such situations, he was rejected by his
successful father, felt himself an outcast, and identified himself
with his mother, in a distorting psychic attachment. For normally
the boy identifies himself with his father. There are two obvious
ways of adjustment in such a predicament: to win the love of the
father or of someone like him—some man, or to destroy the father,
as Oedipus destroyed his father in the story, and to possess the
mother.

The predicament of the male invert is an ambivalence of hostil-
ity and love directed toward the father, the image of authority in
the child's world. There is evidence that Crane attempted in *The
Bridge* a reconciliation with that authority which is equivalent to
the father in the adult world, the established system or way of life.

The Bridge celebrates an American legend and, to some extent, perhaps never without reservations, the forms and achievements of the present age. Particularly significant is the fact that the images embodying Crane's aspiration toward a redeeming order are creations of the current way of life, bridge and airplane.

Perhaps Crane's hindering fear of the sea may likewise be traced to his inversion. In "Voyages, II" death and desire are paired, and the poem ends with the implication that attainment comes only with death, "in the vortex of our grave." Yet if we may venture the Freudian speculation that fear of incest and the vengeful father repelled Crane from the sea, we need not reduce our explanation to that hypothesis. Certainly I would avoid the absurdity of explaining *The Bridge* as a poetic amplification of the phantasies of incest and castration. However determined, Crane's failure to develop his understanding of the 'sea and to submit his concept of the Bridge to the revisions which would have been forced by completed understanding, seems to me to account for the major imperfections of *The Bridge* and for the swift disintegration of the man.

Because he could not endure the descent into chaos, Crane misrepresented the voyage as a wholly conscious adventure. In "Indiana" a young man goes to sea, apparently to return unchanged, bringing nothing new. In "Atlantis" the poet envisaging the Bridge as ship, harp, altar, looks upward in worship and aspiration, and at the end, pathetically enquiring "Is it Cathay?" he remains "floating" becalmed on the terror and temptation of the sea to which he has never wholly committed himself. In "Cape Hatteras" ambivalent engines symbolic of our mechanical achievement are envisaged as "launched" like ships upon the spiritual way of freedom and love defined by Whitman: they "pass out of sight / To course that span of consciousness thou'st named / The Open Road—"

Apart from Crane's assertions, there is nothing to confirm the notion that the voyage of machinery into blank space is related in any way either to Whitman's ideal of brotherhood or to that detached and serene acceptance of experience, including "the delicious nearby freedom of death," which is the spirit of the "Open Road." Hurtled into the false sea of space, the "vast engines" enter that inane toward which the whole conscious aspiration of the poem is lifted, a sphere of freedom which seems nearly illimitable only because it is virtually empty.

A sounder insight into the meaning of the voyage in air is given earlier in "Cape Hatteras." There the conquest of space by the machine is pictured as a triumph of the established world symbolized particularly by the powerful image of the "Cetus-like . . . Dirigible . . . satellited wide / By convoy planes," those "moon-ferrets" which Crane has called "the dragon's covey"—that is, in the terms of familiar symbolism, the children of the Father as enemy. The following passage details the scouting flight of a plane guided by an ace whose mission is "to conjugate infinity's dim marge—/ Anew . . . !" He is shot down. This successful assault of established power on the pioneer of new insight pictures exactly the personal defeat of Crane the rejected son. There are various suggestions in "Cape Hatteras" that the sky is a sea, place of adventure and search, but it is a sea dominated by the Whale and in it the choice son of the dragon is destroyed. He falls—not into the ocean, but broken to the earth: "beached heap of high bravery!"

It is a striking fact that the conclusion of "Cape Hatteras," in which transmutation of the mechanical way of modern life has been proclaimed but not demonstrated, is followed by a song of agonized appeal and hopeless longing addressed to the "Woman of the South." Like the Southern Cross, a constellation lying, for us, as Cathay did for Crane's Columbus, under the horizon—beneath the sea, she belongs to the waters. Approached in a night voyage in which disintegration is represented as begun but not as completed, she is never found: she and the Southern Cross that watched the night sea are drowned in light, in the return to full consciousness.

Despite his self-deceptions, Crane could not altogether conceal the truth. The sea drew him, in horror and fascination. The intensity and exaltation of "Ave Maria," the splendor of the chant that concludes "The River," indicate that he sensed that his salvation was the sea. The poetry most false to this insight—"Indiana" and the conclusion of "Cape Hatteras"—is his weakest.

Crane's passion for the sea was not repressible for long. It gives his poem an obscure but vital coherence. Most of what has been baffling in the structure of *The Bridge*, including much apparent confusion and discontinuity, is clarified into pattern when understood as a consequence of the vacillation produced by Crane's central longing and revulsion.

These forces operate, unfortunately, without Crane's full understanding. In the mind of the derelict sailor of "Cutty Sark," the poet or his protagonist sees "frontiers gleaming," but immediately questions their existence, envisaging the apparent contrary of "running sands," an image suggesting the flowing chaos of debris,

dead bodies, roots and "silted shale" dragged seaward by the
River. In "The River" the images of disorder contribute to the
whole triumphant imaginative conversion of form into its opposite,
which at last takes on the aspect of a goal and defines itself as the
Gulf; in "Cutty Sark" the disorder is unattractive, a senseless
shifting apparently leading nowhere. Here the sea of earth is
repellent, and when the sailor staggers away to his ship, the poet
is apparently altogether justified in taking his different way, land-
ward over the Bridge. The rest of "Cutty Sark," the "calligramme
of ships" seen by the poet "Walking home across the Bridge," has
superficially the appearance of an afterthought. Crane himself
seems to have had nearly this view of it, since he described the
passage to Otto Kahn as "simply a lyrical apostrophe to a world
of loveliness forever vanished." It is, however, strictly relevant,
being no less than a vision of the poet's ultimate success foregone,
the clipper ships of a "phantom regatta" laden with the "opium
and tea" of China, the spoils of Cathay which he will never reach
because he persists in turning away from the sea.

Repeatedly in *The Bridge* a tone of sadness, depression, or
weariness marks the denial of the sea. At the center of the melan-
choly dearth and decay of "Quaker Hill" stands that American
mansion "old Mizzentop, palatial white / Hostelry," a deserted
and stranded ship. Even more somber is the following encounter
with American life, in "The Tunnel," a subway journey to the
water's edge. Here Poe's City in the Sea, a city of the dead as yet
unsunken beside spiritless waters, symbolizes the deathly arrest
of our civilization sustained by "phonographs of hades in the
brain," "tunnels that re-wind themselves." The journey through
that narrow hell of self-perpetuating disorganization cannot bring
release. Beyond it, however, is open water. Having passed through
the tunnel underworld, the poet emerges beside "the River that is
East," that is Cathay and is, of course, a part of the Atlantic
Ocean. His goal is immediately before him. But though his hands
"drop memory" and lie in the abyss of water, he goes no further,
does not descend into it.

In the final section of *The Bridge*, the terms of fulfillment are
intimated, but not accepted. There the "whitest Flower; . . . Anemone, . . . Atlantis"—the "Atlantis Rose" of "Cutty Sark"—the
flower which like Atlantis lies beneath the water, and which stands
for the Absolute or Eternity, as Crane explained to Otto Kahn, is
called on to "hold thy floating singer late." This is the cosmic
flower, symbol of psychic wholeness, the self-possession of the
soul. How shall it be attained? Not by an excursion into open

space, in boundless aspiration, nor by regression into the past, though the journey lead beyond personal memory into the legendary simplicities of the mind. Since the flower lies beneath the sea, it is to be attained only by descent into the waters. But for reasons already explained that descent was impossible to Crane. At the conclusion of *The Bridge*, having approached the sea many times but never having committed himself to it, the poet—or his protagonist—remains in ambiguous suspension floating at the surface of the water.

It is exactly the position defined in "Voyages, II" where the poet, renouncing every "earthly shore," awaits revelation in a sea death, in "the vortex of our grave." In *The Bridge* Crane struggled to bring about a development beyond that position, but he failed in everything except the confirmation of his fate, the necessity of finding fulfillment in a death by water.

The answer to Crane's final question "Is it Cathay?" is that the flower is indeed Cathay and that the poet has not attained it. Cathay lies at the end of a trial by water. The treasure, the flower Atlantis, must be recovered from the bottom of the sea, by one who is willing and able to descend to it, braving chaos. Perhaps in his ordeal such a one would discover the flower to be precisely the feared act of descent, desertion of the ship and dependence upon the unformulated life of the deeps. And perhaps thereafter he would be seen buoyed on the water, a "floating singer." But there is a great difference between one who floats but who has never entirely entrusted himself to the water and one who floats but has given himself to it. The latter has risen from death. The former is delaying death, and his reprieve is his defeat.

Crane ceased to write much, his life lost force and meaning. Apparently not wholeheartedly, he attempted suicide, choosing poison first. Then at last he found his way: suicide by leaping from the deck of the *Orizaba*, into the Gulf where he had already drowned so much. The *Orizaba* became his bridge into the sea. What he could not do directly and fully as an artist, he did in his symbolic death: he found his way to the waters. But it was an imperfect attainment.

Stanley K. Coffman, Jr.

Symbolism in *The Bridge*

A great deal has been said about the failure of Hart Crane's
The Bridge.[1] I should like here to add a note upon an aspect of
The Bridge which, as far as I know, has not been more than mentioned, probably because the finality of the usual criticism of the
poem tends to obscure it. Perhaps the shortest way to what I
propose is through Ezra Pound's definition of the Image: "that
which presents an intellectual and emotional complex in an instant
of time."[2] As symbol providing a logical meaning for the poem,
the Bridge has been examined and judgment delivered; but the
pattern of language through which Crane hoped to make his symbol effective as intellectual and emotional complex, or, to use his
terminology, a "new *word*, never before spoken and impossible to
actually enunciate,"[3] has been left almost untouched.

Reprinted by permission of the Modern Language Association of America
from *PMLA*, LXVI (March 1951), 65-77. Copyright © 1951 by the Modern
Language Association of America.
[1] *The Collected Poems of Hart Crane,* ed. with an Introd. by Waldo Frank
(New York, 1946).
[2] "A Few Don'ts by an Imagiste," *Poetry.* I, vi (March 1913), 200.
[3] "General Aims and Theories." See Philip Horton, *Hart Crane* (New York,
1937), p. 327 (App. I).

The remark has frequently been made that the Bridge as object lent itself admirably to the symbolic use Crane meant it to serve: its qualities were just those which could be translated into the metaphors that would express concretely the central abstractions of his poem. His belief in the continuous, organic growth of human history, in which each period is a source of the next; or his idea that the American, and particularly the modern, industrial American, period is to lift us over into an even greater future; or the purpose he sees in the poem itself, which is to link the reader, and the poet, to their own past, present, and future—all are effectively objectified in the figure of the Bridge. Again, each of the several human achievements dealt with in the poem may, by the nature of Crane's (and Whitman's) myth, be seen symbolically as bridge: Columbus' voyage of discovery, the transcontinental routes of the frontier settlers, and then the accomplishments of industrial science exemplified in the national highway and railway, and the airplane.

This, however, leaves the symbol to be apprehended only in terms of concepts, leaves it, in fact, with only the kind of logic Crane wanted his poetry to replace. The Bridge was not just to symbolize a particular belief but to reproduce all the qualities of experiencing that belief; it was to fuse the intellectual and emotional components of a belief so completely that the poem as a whole, dominated by this symbol, would become metaphor translating this particular aspect of the poet's consciousness. There is, for example, the pattern of language which conveys an exhilaration that is part of Crane's mysticism and grows out of an imaginative approach to the Bridge as object: the Bridge is seen vaulting the sea (transcending and including it, but with the transcending and including expressed in such a way that they can be felt); its counterpart, the highway, *leaps* from Far Rockaway to Golden Gate; the railway *strides* the dew, *straddles* the hill; the wires *span* the mountain stream—each verb giving the symbolic action human and therefore immediately apprehensible character. Emphasizing further the religious and emotional, the Bridge's outline suggests an "arching path/Upward," an image repeated in "arching strands of song" and "spiring cordage." In the *sweep* of the Bridge, in the petition that its "lariat sweep encinctured" descend and enfold us within its embrace, Crane is further drawing upon the affective powers of the object. The Bridge is Love's paradigm, revealing its inflected forms (aspiration, exhilaration, all-inclusiveness) through the motions of spanning, spiring, sweeping, which evoke these feelings.

The Bridge is also "arc synoptic," which not only strengthens the religious connotations, but shows how closely Crane was allying himself with the particular mysticism that was Whitman's religion. Like the concept of reality as Love, this of the object as microcosm recalls Whitman, but where Whitman is content to allow philosophic conviction to carry the poetry and thus strings out his catalogues of metonyms, Crane turns his belief in philosophic unity into a technique of expression, somewhat in the manner of the French Symbolists, and unifies his poem by showing how the universe will repeat its patterns and images, especially one so expressive as that discovered in the configuration of the Bridge. Love itself surveys the world with a *"diametric* gaze"; the world is God's "teeming *span."* Both day and night reveal the Bridge's form: night is a "sapphire *wheel,"* dawn appears as "dayspring's spreading *arc,"* and the Bridge lifts night to day's *"cycloramic* crest." The planes of Cape Hatteras are launched into "abysmal cupolas of space." The larger phenomena of nature reflect this basic configuration in other ways; one notes, for example, the rainbow's arch, an image that occurs at four widely separated places in the poem, the crescent of the moon, which images the actual planet, the "hair's keen crescent" of Pocahontas, and the earth, a "crescent ring . . . zoned with . . . fire."

"Proem" opens, in fact, with the flight of the gull, whose wings trace "white rings of tumult" and who disappears from sight with "inviolate curve," a spiring, sweeping motion which is intensified by the sudden contrast with the "chained bay waters" and which inevitably merges into and enforces the qualities of the Bridge's own *curveship.* In "The River," carrying out the pattern, eyeless fish *curvet,* and in "Ave Maria," the sails are mustered in "holy rings," just as the image of "Pennants, parabolas" reappears in appropriate guise in "Cutty Sark." Ironically, the same motion is repeated in the horror of man's machine world, concentrated in the subway hell of "The Tunnel": as the car rounds a bend for the dive under the river, newspapers on the cluttered floor "wing, revolve and wing." All nature writes the figure of the curve or, by extension, the circle; and the universality of its appearance adds persuasiveness to the symbolic meaning of the Bridge. The Bridge thus speaks, through this one of its properties, a universal geometry, an "unfractioned idiom," and argues, by what can best be called a logic of metaphor, the fundamental point which the poem was to present: its man-made configuration, repeated by nature, is given a kind of divinity, and the mathematical thinking which planned it a like sanctity.

There are also passages in which Crane is working not from the Bridge into nature but from the Bridge into the civilization of the Twentieth Century. The bird of "Proem" becomes the plane of "Cape Hatteras," and something of the weakness of the latter section is apparent in a comparison of the two. There are lines of "Cape Hatteras" where the metaphor, translating the plane's flight into the language of geometry, has the strength of the metaphorical process in "Proem": wings clipping "the last *peripheries* of light," or tracing in the "bright *circumferences*" of the sky "marauding *circles*," or outlining a "rapid *helix*" in their ascent, speak with some economy and conviction. As is frequently pointed out, however, Crane is not content with individual metaphors and tries to overwhelm with verbs of motion, wheeling, surging, twisting, banking, spinning, and so on, until he blurs and confuses an effect that should be as sharp and clean as the "oilrinsed *circles*" of the bearings.

As bridge between the circling, spiring motion of these central figures, the bird in "Proem" and the plane in "Cape Hatteras," Crane has used "The Dance," which presents the ecstasy of union between the protagonist as Maquokeeta and Pocahontas, the earth of America. Man and nature here become one, and the preparation for union, the tribal dance, in itself suggests an abandon like that expressed in the eulogy of flight. The water now weaves "laughing chains" and the protagonist sees smoke *swirling* through the "yellow chestnut glade." In Maquokeeta's "turbine crest," a cyclone *threshes*; as the dance proceeds to its climax, the "oak grove *circles* in a crash of leaves"; and the dance ends as Maquokeeta has *folded* the "strong prayer" in his arms. Considering the opportunities for expanding this particular pattern of imagery, however, "The Dance" actually adds very little except by implication. This may be as Crane planned, and it avoids the excesses of "Cape Hatteras"; but it may also have a significance to be understood when one discovers the kind of imagery which *does* dominate this section, imagery which, though allied to the transcendent, is still of the earth.

As several of the quotations have implied, Crane goes beyond the universal language of geometry to show the unity between science and nature. In "Cape Hatteras," wounds from the "screaming petals" of grenades are wrapped with *theorems*—our viciously homeopathic way of treating what seems here to be modern disease. As the grenade fragments are petals, so the theorems are sharp as *hail*, indicating the process by which the world of nature and the world of science and industry become interchangeable, the process which in "The Tunnel" works toward the collapse of the conviction it is supposed to express, when the horror of the machine becomes apparent largely through this very effort to see it as human. Thunder that is *galvothermic* and "synergy of waters" carry us even farther afield than the general vocabulary of geometry, but Crane does not often stray from the principal source of the dominant imagery. The unity of natural and man-made, as seen in the universality of geometric imagery, occurs with such frequency that one hardly notices the process in "the Square, the Circle burning bright," even though Crane has prepared for it some twenty lines earlier with "Times Square to Columbus Circle."

He abstracts, then, from the Bridge properties of motion (implicit) and of configuration. The motion evokes directly feelings which accompany the function of the symbol as "Cognizance"; to inspire, to embrace, to exhilarate; the configuration evokes less directly, but after its universality is shown, after it becomes a fundamental pattern of the Universe revealing unity and linking scientific thought with the Universal plan, its evocative powers are similar. Crane also abstracts a property which perhaps has even greater evocative powers; from the opening image of the gull shedding *"white* rings of tumult" in the harbor *dawns*, the imagery of light plays through the poem.

The further one goes in investigating the nature of Crane's symbol, the more urgently he feels the attraction Whitman seems to have held for Crane. It is not simply a matter of one poet providing another with a myth that will enable him to accept his present and his past—that will alleviate the torment of isolation; it goes much deeper than this and demonstrates, at least for this one poem, that even the feelings which accompany intuitive understanding are to be expressed in imagery clearly reminiscent of Whitman's. More than a suggestion of this appeared in the discussion of Crane's emphasis upon the kinetic, but it can be seen conclusively, I think, as one examines this further component of the Bridge's symbolic meaning and its development through the poem.

He uses images both of light and of whiteness; the color, however, seems secondary and functions mainly to produce certain feelings which are essential to the light symbolism and which light itself would probably not convey. Light is not only symbolic of vision, revelation, but, in sense, *is* the revelation; and it is the revelation of Whitman's "Passage to India":

O Thou transcendent,
Nameless, the fibre and the breath,
Light of the light,

where light is Truth and the human discoveries which reveal the Truth, and where the light flooding the century of science is contrasted with the darkness of the Past—"the dark unfathom'd retrospect." Probably more effectively than any of his poems, "Passage to India" employs the contrasts of light and shadow that Whitman mentions so frequently in one of his favored words, *chiaroscuro*. It is this poem from which Crane quotes in *The Bridge* and from which radiate Whitman's eyes "bright with myth," the light that suffuses *The Bridge*.

The light of *The Bridge* is predominantly the light of dawn. "Proem" opens on a dawn setting. Columbus, recounting his discovery, says he waited "Till dawn" should reveal the new continent, which he finally saw, the palms chevroning "the first lighted hill." The love scene which begins Section II occurs in a harbor dawn as the "pallid air" gradually gives way to full daylight. In "The Dance" the poet sets out on his search for Pocahontas as he sees the crescent moon die, then a single star take its place in the sky where it remains until it bleeds "into the dawn"; with this one might compare the closing lines of "The Harbor Dawn," the last stanza of "Atlantis," and, finally, Whitman's descriptions of the dawn in *Specimen Days*.[4] The dawn image reappears, though not as prominently, in "Cutty Sark," as a moment of calm after the night in the waterfront dive; in "Cape Hatteras," but only in phrases often lost in the verbiage of this section: "auroral beaches"; "dawn patrol"; Whitman "pallid there as chalk" and evasive as "dayspring's spreading arc"; the planes, "Easters of speeding light." Crane refers to the dawn in "The Tunnel," though with entirely different effect: of the Daemon's influence he exclaims:

---

4 "The character of the heralded morning, ineffably sweet and fresh and limpid, but for the esthetic sense alone, and for purity without sentiment. I have itemized the night—but dare I attempt the cloudless dawn? (What subtle tie is this between one's soul and the break of day? Alike, and yet no two nights or morning shows ever exactly alike.) Preceded by an immense star, almost unearthly in its effusion of white splendor, with two or three long unequal spoke-rays of diamond radiance shedding down through the fresh morning air below—an hour of this, and then the sunrise." *Complete Prose Works* (Boston, 1901), p. 112. See also p. 113.

> O cruelly to inoculate the brinking dawn
> With antennae toward worlds that glow and sink;—

which brings together contrasting images of light, two ways in which the world may be seen. Again in the Daemon's presence, the dawn is the "muffled slaughter of a day in birth."

On the literal level, the color of dawn corresponds to the color of the Bridge. In "The Harbor Dawn" it is a time of contemplation when the sounds of man's civilization are muffled and indistinct. Here, and in "Ave Maria," it is associated with discovery and with love. It is also a preparation for greater light, and in each of the scenes in which it appears there is motion as day breaks with the rising of the sun. It seems a natural counterpart to the Bridge, enforcing the suggestive qualities of the latter and repeating its abstract meaning: dawn is another bridge.

Dawn and the "Steeled Cognizance" share another property. "Proem" places the steel Bridge against the background of snow submerging "an iron year." Later, Crane describes the dawn sky as "*cool* feathery fold," and the window in this scene "frostily clears." Coolness is frequently emphasized elsewhere in images of snow, rime. The setting just mentioned develops a related imagery in the "gongs in *white* surplices," "*beshrouded* wails," "soft *sleeves* of sound," "*pillowed* bay," epithets which not only refer to sleep but express, in their connotation of the coolness of passion spent, the purity of the dawn and of the poet's vision. In certain of the words quoted, however, there is a suggestion of eeriness which seems a faint echo of Melville's chapter on the whiteness of the whale; the old sailor says, for example, "that damned *white Arctic* killed my time . . ." There is also a suggestion of softness, which the Bridge will not offer—except in the reflected light of the moon.

The clear, cool, white light of the Bridge is further reflected, as its arc is reflected, by nature and by man; its "secular light" permeates our being, is "the bright drench and fabric of our veins." The sea gull can be seen to repeat its color, its coolness ("cold gulls"), as well as its configuration; the albatross, once flashing into a line, has a similar effect. The "glittering Pledge" of Deity also has natural counterparts in the stars, with which it appears most frequently in the poem's closing section; in the moonlight, which covers it in this same final poem; and in the clouds, to which Crane returns five or six times for imagery. Other, brief flashes of nature's white occur: "the *mistletoe* of dreams," the "nervous shark tooth" swinging from the old sailor's chain, the "theorems sharp as *hail*" (indicating the multiple values of the most efficient of Crane's images). One recurrent image of this kind is especially worth noting as an instance of the technique Crane has used to give force to his symbol and as further indication of parallel between his technique and Whitman's. He several times comes back to the word *foam,* whose motion and color both contribute to the symbolic pattern in a peculiarly effective way. The image is seen first in the words, "stag teeth foam about the raven throat," which, in their contrasting colors, emphasize whiteness (cf. the same contrast in "Glacial sierras and the flight of ravens"). But it is carried over into "Cutty Sark," where the clipper ships are "scarfed of *foam*"; then into "Cape Hatteras," where the poet speaks of the "captured fume of space" which *foams* in our ears, and of the "sky's pancreas of *foaming* anthracite." In the same section, it is repeated in "Cowslips and shad-blow, flaked like tethered *foam*/Around bared teeth of stallions" (followed almost immediately by "breakers cliffward leaping"). The image, suggesting a motion almost frenzied, and the color of dawn and vision, serves in a double capacity to increase the impact of the central symbol.

One finds the color extended, as Crane extended the configuration, into man's world as well as nature's. Traffic lights, *lights* of cars skim across the Bridge at night (man's light, like the reflected light of the moon, visible only at night). Still in "Proem," the reader imagines the flickering of white against black in the cinema, and a line or two later sees the white of its screen; and man's white appears in the *"shrill shirt"* of the suicide tilting upon the Bridge's parapets. There is the phantasy of the protagonist at his office desk in the city which brings to his mind *sails* crossing the *page* of figures; the whiteness of the paper has been blurred by the figures, images of rational, abstract thought, but reappears in the color of the sails. Both gull and sails in this environment are *apparitional,* though both occur again as the poem progresses, the sails in "Ave Maria" mustered "in *holy rings.*"

This use of the color in the context of the man-made seems to suggest only reflected light or the shrillness noted above, and in "Cape Hatteras" Crane employs color in such a way as to counteract these overtones. Here "The bearings glint, . . . shined/In oil-rinsed circles of blind ecstasy!"; here the "razor sheen" of the *silver* plane, the "larval-*silvered* hangars," are a kind of whiteness which, not only in color but coolness (and in the spiring, arching) reinforces the splendor of the Bridge, repeats its color and the color of the dawn, and borrows for this achievement of the machine age the affective powers of the central religious symbol, at the same time enlarging its area of meaning. That the imagery of light is intended to represent all of man's works is clear, I think, from such phrases as "frontiers *gleaming* of his mind," but that the deprecatory overtones cannot be wholly dispelled is hinted by the question that follows: "or are there frontiers—running sands sometimes." While our lives appear as "long wake of phosphor,/ iridiscent," this is also "trailed derision." While the Bridge is "white, pervasive Paradigm" of Love, and Anemone, "whitest Flower," its light in "Atlantis" is that of the moon. And, a small point, but perhaps of even more immediate significance, the smile the poet's mother "almost brought me once from church" flickers "through the *snow* screen." Whiteness in *The Bridge* shades not only into the still clarity, coolness and vision of dawn, but into the blankness of the frozen ("occult snows"), approaching the quality of Melville's white horror, the negation of Whitman's Love and light.

One more instance of Crane's use of white, to illustrate further the multiple values of his imagery. We have seen how the stars become, by their color and light, by their suggestions of coolness (and perhaps, now, of remoteness) natural counterparts to the Bridge. In "Atlantis" the stars ring the Bridge in a *"palladium* helm." Silver-white *palladium* from the vocabulary of science carries out, of course, Crane's effort to express the natural in the vocabulary of his age (with *helm*, it gives new expression to the old); it is an element which is rare, costly; it is malleable and fuses more readily than the others of its group—all properties which support and enlarge the meaning of the central symbol to which it is related through its color and its use here with *star*. It was, in fact, named for an asteroid, which in turn took its name from Pallas Athene. *Palladium* also denotes a statue of Athene, in particular one on the citadel of Troy which was supposed to guarantee the safety of the city, and by extension applies to anything that is said to ensure protection: a further passage from palladium to the Bridge, and additional evidence of the remarkable strength of Crane's epithets.

Light, however, is not only the cool or chill whiteness which adheres to the Bridge; there is through the poem a contrasting light, and both the contrast and the underlying similarity of the two kinds of color imagery are germane to the poem's theme. Light is also fire and is introduced in "Proem" by the image of the noon sun, a "rip-tooth of the sky's acetylene" which "leaks" from girder into street (repeating the downward motion of the

elevator with meaning that later becomes clear). The sun is reflected by man's world in "window-eyes aglitter" disking the sun
("The Harbor Dawn") and in windows gleaming at "sunset"
("Quaker Hill"). Columbus' soliloquy opens with the "sun's red
caravel" dropping light behind him, and thus making the contrast
he notes between his immediate situation and the morning of the
newly discovered land he has left. The soliloquy, in fact, presents
the whole world as, from Columbus' view, "Sun-cusped and zoned
with . . . fire." The sunset here merges into night, but as Columbus continues his monologue he images God in terms of the fire
which stands out of the darkness. God, according to Columbus,
reveals himself through the corposant (with its inevitable suggestion of *Moby Dick*), through the flame of Teneriffe's garnet, and
is addressed in the climactic final line of the section as "Thou
Hand of Fire." It is evident that for Columbus, at least, God in
one guise is scourge to man, and the sea which can yet destroy his
ships and cut off from the world the knowledge of discovery is
thus appropriately the flaming sunset sea, though because of his
discovery and vision it is a "modulated fire" with the color of
pearls.

The fire's red has a beauty here, as it has in its next important
context, the body, the red flesh of Pocahontas. Red and white
merge momentarily in this section, for it involves the love scene
with the woman who disappears and the search for whom leads
the poet to Pocahontas and the dance. A marginal note points to
the equation of red here with flesh, with passion, and ultimately
with the earth. "The Dance," which leads to union of Maquokeeta's flesh with that of the Indian girl, crackles with fire imagery,
the atmosphere of "the furious noon":

> And every tendon scurries toward the twangs
> Of lightning deltaed down your saber hair.
> Now snaps the flint in every tooth; red fangs
> And splay tongues thinly busy the blue air . . .
>
> Wrapped in that fire, I saw more escorts wake—
> Flickering, sprint up the hill groins like a tide.
>
> I heard the hush of lava wrestling your arms,
> And stag teeth foam about the raven throat;
> Flame cataracts of heaven in seething swarms
> Fed down your anklets to the sunset's moat.

The color of flame is defined by varying hues in the poem. It
may be the tawny blond of windows lighted by an early sun, as in

"The Harbor Dawn"; or it may be the color of maize: "The far/ Hushed gleaming fields and pendant seething wheat/Of knowledge, . . . /The kindled crown!" It may be the mustard color of the River, whose glow is also "undertowed sunlight." But it is basically associated with knowledge, passion, or love *known to man.* As the course of American life and history, the historic consciousness of America, the River is addressed as Passion. Fire is beauty but also a scourge, the scourge of mortality, the limitations of space and time, the eagle and the serpent (described elsewhere as "sunning inch of unsuspecting fibre— . . . as clean as fire"). The effort of *The Bridge* is to express the conquest of space and time, which is accomplished symbolically in "The Dance," and show the common source of the two kinds of light, a sanctified white and earthly red, to go beyond the materialistic half-truth of the hoboes who simply attribute change and destruction to "fire and snow."

That this is the principal meaning of the contrasting images of light seems clear not only from "The Dance," from the reference to the eyes of the human prophet Whitman, which *blaze* with "love's own diametric gaze," but mainly from the use of this imagery in "Atlantis." The Bridge, the myth, is "whitest Flower," with "fell unshadow," but is upborne through "the bright drench and fabric of our veins"; it is the "stallion glow" of the stars. In the closing lines there occurs the image of the "star/That bleeds infinity"; and the Bridge is "One Song, one Bridge of Fire!"

The imagery of fire, however, lights up scenes in which fire is the destroyer. In "Cape Hatteras" one watches a "Sunward Escadrille," but this machinery is also employed to "fly/War's fiery kennel." Most striking, though, is Crane's adaptation of it in "The Tunnel," where one sees not fire, but the waste products of its destructive force. Here the worlds only "glow and sink"; there is thunder, but without lightning; love is a "burnt match skating in a urinal"; and Poe appears in these lines:

> Whose head is swinging from the swollen strap?
> Whose body *smokes* along the bitten rails,
> Bursts from a *smoldering* bundle far behind
> In back forks of the chasms of the brain,—
> *Puffs* from a riven stump far out behind
> In interborough fissures of the mind . . . ?

It is through the Bridge that our eyes are to be lifted beyond time, but it will be "through smoking pyres of love and death."

Thus Columbus' concept of God as "Thou Hand of Fire," and its echo in "The Tunnel":

> Kiss of our agony Thou gatherest,
> O Hand of Fire
> gatherest—

Love is passion, the light of fire, and mortal; but it is God-given and though it brings agony, it is also the way to God and a white light without the ambiguous dross of mortality. One merges into the other, one is necessary to the other; "High unto Labrador the sun strikes free/Her speechless dream of snow."

Clearly this Bridge is not a symbol in the conventional sense, as an object which can, by virtue of certain properties, be translated into terms of an abstraction. Crane has conceived of it rather as the French Symbolists did, working out, for example, correspondences between the object and other phenomena of the natural or civilized world, and between the object and a state of consciousness existing in the poet. Crane's *word* is, in fact, on the evidence offered by *The Bridge*, very clearly Mallarmé's: "Le vers qui de plusieurs vocables refait un mot total, neuf, étranger à la langue et comme incantatoire, achève cet isolement de la parole: ... et vous cause cette surprise de n'avoir ouï jamais tel fragment ordinaire d'élocution."[5] That it becomes metaphor (or myth as the Symbolists understood it) for a complex state may perhaps be confirmed by a glance at a further pattern of imagery through which it speaks to the reader. "Atlantis" opens with an epigraph from Plato, "Music is then the knowledge of that which relates to love in harmony and system," and the use of this quotation seems to parallel Symbolist insistence upon the musical potentialities of language and upon approximating poetry to music. There was a generous measure of Platonism in Symbolist theorizing about the aims of poetry, and the function of music as suggesting the harmony of the Ideal world figured largely in this theorizing. Though the poetry of *The Bridge* seldom approaches music in the Symbolist manner, through special attention to the pitch and rhythm of language, Crane reveals a correspondence between his symbol and an Aeolian harp whose music by its harmony recalls the harmony between man and his universe, the harmony within the universal plan.

---

[5] Introd. to R. Ghil, *Traité du Verbe.* Quoted by Guy Michaud, *La Doctrine Symboliste (Documents)* (Paris, 1947), pp. 26–27.

As Brom Weber has pointed out, Crane prepares for this climactic transformation of his symbol in "Proem," where the Bridge
is "harp and altar," whose choiring strings could not have been
aligned by mere toil of man.[6] (It is *altar* as bridge between human
and divine.) Other musical reference is infrequent until the closing
section. The distance of the highway's span and the pleasure felt
in its sweep are conveyed through the *hurdy-gurdy* that grinds
out the miles and whose sound winds down "gold arpeggios"
(suggesting also a sense of motion and motion upward); here,
however, the grind organ serves mainly, as it does in Eliot's "Portrait of a Lady," to recall another world to the protagonist. The
planes of "Cape Hatteras" are "Up-chartered choristers" whose
song theoretically would be the universal harmony of the Bridge's
song. The escalator in "The Tunnel" "lifts a serenade," but
"Stilly/ Of shoes, umbrellas, each eye attending its shoe"; the
waters of the River are an oily tympanum, an image less aural
probably than visual.

But in "Atlantis" the music imagery is dominant, fusing the
other patterns that have been mentioned and giving them a
greater intensity than they have had before in the poem. Here the
Bridge is not only harp but accompaniment to "Sibylline voices"
which "waveringly stream/As though a god were issue of the
strings. . . ." The Bridge is light, motion, sound:

> O Thou
> Whose canticle fresh chemistry assigns
> To rapt inception and beatitude,—
> Always through blinding cables, to our joy,
> Of thy white seizure springs the prophecy:
> Always through spiring cordage, pyramids
> Of silver sequel, Deity's young name
> Kinetic of white choiring wings . . . ascends.

There are "orphic strings," entrancing, Dionysian, and thus
mystic, oracular (Sibylline). But Orpheus (though his music
saved the Argonauts from the lure of the Sirens) appears not
without connotations of tragedy for, almost in sight of the upper
regions, he turned back to look at Eurydice, and thus lost her.

[6] *Hart Crane* (New York, 1948), p. 337. In the same passage Weber quotes
the following comment about *The Bridge* made by Crane to Waldo Frank:
"I have attempted to induce the same feelings of elation, etc.—like being
carried forward and upward simultaneously—both in imagery, rhythm and
repetition, that one experiences in walking across my beloved Brooklyn
Bridge . . ."

Intended or not, this overtone of meaning agrees with the questioning of these final lines: "Is it Cathay . . . ?"; and the last image leaves considerable doubt concerning the mystic or any but the ecstatic quality of the poet's or the Bridge's song. It is a song suspended in air: "Whispers antiphonal in azure swing."

These, then, appear to be the chief components of the Bridge as Image or *word*. There are one or two minor ones, like the terminology of castles, moats, tournaments, of medieval rather than modern ordnance, which are a much less effective means of enlarging the perspective and significance of the contemporary scene, a not too subtle device to dignify the machine; yet the bristling spears of "The Dance," the bright steel of each plane as a "hurtling javelin," and the keen, cutting quality of the Bridge imaged as "blade on tendon blade" do add important strength and meaning to the *word*. Or the colors which supplement the imagery of light, particularly the azures, blues, cobalts, which have a slightly more functional place in the poem, as in "The Dance," where the blue hills of earth reflect the blue of heaven.

There are, of course, dangers in the approach that I have used. It tends to isolate the symbol, whereas Crane in most cases works his symbolic pattern carefully into the texture of the separate sections. It does not measure the extent to which his effort in this direction falls short of success; where his interest in a passage wavers, the effectiveness of the Bridge imagery wavers.[7] Yet it does reinforce the accepted criticism of the poem, showing, particularly in his use of images of whiteness, more than a hint of undesirable ambiguity, an uneasy juxtaposition of Whitman's "light" and Melville's "white"; and, at the same time, in the imagery of fire in its various forms the concept which he apparently depended upon to resolve this contradictory view of the transcendental real. The primary value of this approach, however, is in its emphasis upon Crane's brilliant elaboration of symbolic meaning, even though the brilliance is vitiated by failure to cope

---

[7] Through "Indiana" there runs the imagery of gold, contrasting with other instances of this color—the rich gold of maize, the fire of the setting sun, and of earthly passion—but while the Gold Rush may be justifiable here historically, Crane's rather casual use of it to signify the illusory and sordid nature of the mercenary ideal is as hackneyed and sentimental as the situation which is the basis for this section. Yet note that the circular motion of the dance with its indirect relation to the Bridge and thus to the ecstasy of the mystic's intuition, is ironically repeated in the gyrations of the burlesque queen in "National Winter Garden"; "Southern Cross" uses the imagery of light (the cool silver of dawn and of the stars, the other light of fire "slowly smoldering"), and "Virginia" turns this light into gold as it turns the ideal woman into the average modern girl.

philosophically with his material. While the qualities of the symbol do not evenly permeate the poem, while the symbol itself betrays its confusion, one ought not attempt an estimate of *The Bridge* without understanding Crane's grasp of a fundamental Symbolist technique.

John R. Willingham

"Three Songs" of Hart Crane's
The Bridge: A Reconsideration

Critics have often professed a failure to see much justification for Part V, or "Three Songs," in the structural pattern of Hart Crane's major poem, *The Bridge*—a poem considered by many to be one of the major artistic achievements of the twentieth century. Coming as the songs do after the exalted hymn of praise (or "ode to Whitman," as Crane described "Cape Hatteras"), these lyrics have seemed to certain explicators of the poem to violate Crane's intention to achieve an epic for modern America. Brom Weber has called the lyrics "unnecessary" and has complained that they "further increase the logical disintegration of *The Bridge*."[1] Hyatt Waggoner's viewpoint is similar, and his analysis of the poem suggests that "Three Songs" duplicates the "deflation" of "Quaker Hill."[2] Howard Moss presumably includes this fifth section in his dismissal of the entire poem.[3] But I wish to suggest that there are

From *American Literature,* XXVII (March 1955), 62-68. Reprinted by permission of the journal and the author.
[1] Brom Weber, *Hart Crane* (New York, 1948), pp. 367, 370.
[2] Hyatt Howe Waggoner, *The Heel of Elohim: Science and Values in Modern American Poetry* (Norman, Okla., 1950), p. 185.
[3] Howard Moss, "Disorder as Myth: Hart Crane's *The Bridge*," *Poetry,* LXII, 32-43 (April, 1943).

good grounds for seeing "Three Songs"—and indeed the entire poem—as a cut above the failure which it has been branded by critical platitude.

Several things should be kept in mind about the function and tone of "Cape Hatteras." Following "Cutty Sark," the "ode to Whitman" had to try in some measure to answer the query— "where can you be/*Nimbus?* and you rivals two"—with which "Cutty Sark" ended. The long walk home across the bridge started the often disappointed protagonist, depressed anew from his experience with the old sailor, to thinking about the promise of America as symbolized in the exploits of the brilliant Yankee clippers. This quandary over the contradiction of pioneer vision and material fact is quite natural; indeed, the effort to resolve the conflict has been the impetus of the entire quest of the protagonist across the time and space of America. The fact that his mind is turning over again this pivotal question as he walks across the bridge is in keeping, of course, with the religious function of the bridge symbol as it is evoked in "Proem." The bridge quite naturally and organically, as it turns out, directs the thought of the wanderer to Whitman, Crane's symbol of America's mystical vision.

The evocation of Whitman in "Cape Hatteras" assists the pro-tagonist to answer the question: the dream of the clipper ships is still alive. The new American conquests of space, celebrated by Whitman in "Passage to India" and "The Prayer of Columbus," reassure the protagonist that the mystic essence of America is still active. As the epigraph of "Cape Hatteras" suggests, the particular mission of the great ships, as indeed of all historical movements, may be finished: but the mystic impulse which built the bridge, lured Columbus westward, and sent the forty-niners on the trail to El Dorado, is kept vital in the spatial achievements of the twentieth century. In the spiritual union with the older poet, the protagonist is able to hold onto, even transcend, the memory of the virgin physical beauty of America which had been celebrated earlier in "The River" and "The Dance." But these physical beauties are given a new meaning through the encounter with Whitman, and that new meaning is achieved by the transfigur-ation of love. As the section ends, the protagonist takes a sacred vow never to abandon the vision of Whitman—a kind of vision made even more congenial for Crane by his reading of Waldo Frank's *Our America* (1919) and William Carlos Williams's *In the American Grain* (1925).

It is true, as Weber has said, that there is certainly a change of mood from "Cape Hatteras" to "Three Songs"; but I shall suggest that the change is intentional and not damaging to the poem as a whole as Weber has thought. If one remembers that for several years before and during the composition of *The Bridge* Crane had been much attracted and influenced by the critical theories and writing style of Waldo Frank, it can be seen more clearly, I think, what Crane has attempted and accomplished in "Three Songs" and why this section is organically sound. Frank's most characteristic and successful device in such novels as *City Block* (1922) and *Not Heaven* (1953) has been the stringing together of a series of apparently unrelated episodes which in reality have a close interdependence. A careful examination of Frank's best work will show that the structure of his novels offers an analogy to that of a symphony: a theme is stated, a countertheme follows, and the whole is finally resolved in another movement. Such a method is essentially that followed by Whitman; thus it had a double validity for Crane's purposes in *The Bridge*.

Having been permitted through the beneficent ministry of the bridge to move beyond the experience of the lost and bewildered sailor of "Cutty Sark" into the ecstatic avowal of "Cape Hatteras," the protagonist is attempting to apply in the first of the songs "Southern Cross," Whitman's lesson to the sailor's night journey through dark waters. Meaning must be found here, or the protagonist will drown in the chaos of the sea; the bridge will turn out to be a cruel hoax. "Cape Hatteras" carried a strong hint, as did "Ave Maria" and "Harbor Dawn" earlier, that a religious synthesis of the problems of modern America can be attained by the key of love. The identity of the star is not clear to the sailor-protagonist at first, he is certain only that it is a female for he asks whether it be "Eve! Magdalene!/or Mary, you?" This female turns out to be Eve, for it is on the lowest level—sexual love—that love as the unifying principle of all historical movement and achievement must be understood first. If the protagonist emerges from this experience with clearer understanding, he will be ready to move through Magdalene to Mary in his search for the truth which love can reveal. The sailor complains to the Eve-principle as suggested by the constellation of the Southern Cross that completely satisfying physical love is hard to obtain in the modern world and that Pocahontas's pledge of abundant and rich love for the American seeker has not been redeemed. The female is blamed for the failure of the union which

the protagonist so fervently desires. However, the irony of his plea
lies in the fact that the sailor, presumably identified with that of
"Cutty Sark," has wandered away from the loving soil of America;
lacking insight, he has expended the restlessness (the movement
of God) within him on the wrong pursuits (i.e., an obsessive
materialism). He cannot find love because he has not love within
himself. Eve cannot return to the garden until Adam seeks her
with real love instead of mere desire.

Having gained some insight into the lack of satisfaction in love
in the case of the sailor, the protagonist passes on to consider in
"National Winter Garden" the place of the female and of love in
the urban hell of New York, within the shadow of the mighty
bridge. Eve is left behind in "Southern Cross" for an encounter
with a modern Magdalene, a sleazy dancer who is seen as the
priestess of love which has been mechanized into lust. But we
must remember that the Magdalene of the New Testament could
become a means to show men the way to spiritual redemption, in
spite of what men thought she was. Throughout this song Crane
emphasizes the essential connection of the twentieth-century burlesque queen with certain aspects of Pocahontas. Through their
womanhood both possess the means of resolving the chaos by
bringing male restlessness (Columbus, Rip Van Winkle, the
hoboes, the sailor) to fruition and unity. The dancer yet bears
some traces of the Pocahontas of the richly significant and mythic
tribal dance: she wears the jewels of Pocahontas ("her silly snake
rings" and "turquoise fakes"), even though they have degenerated
in beauty and meaning. She contains a vital connection with the
physical world of Pocahontas, the pioneer, and modern man. In
the movements of her hands and hips the snake and eagle symbols
of "The Dance" remain though, again, they have lost their former
tribal significance. But the traces of meaning are still there, for
the dance mirrors man's desire and quest for love and unity even
if the desire is burlesqued. Nothing in the quest of man since
Columbus has been lost; all is contained in the movements of the
dancer which are "the burlesque of our lust" but also, significantly, our "faith." The two can never be completely separated,
the wondering and soon to be purged protagonist realizes. Again,
what is required is the application of the Whitmanesque vision to
see through all the apparent degeneracy and cheapness into the
essential beauty and fertility which are America's heritage. There
is a double significance intended in the closing lines of the section,
I think, which emphasizes the advance in understanding represented by this part of the poem. It is true that the sexual

excitement evoked by the dancer lugs contemporary man back "lifeward" to the impending hell, but it is to a life which can yet be reclaimed and redeemed if vision is achieved. This is certainly preferable to the death and sterility accepted by the sailor of "Cutty Sark" and "Southern Cross." The trappings and cavortings of the modern Magdalene are clues or "signals" which can be as efficacious for the penitent protagonist as the muffled sounds of "Harbor Dawn" or the clanging gong of the subway in "The Tunnel." They are means of working one's way out of the labyrinth of time and space into the light of a present made significant by the bridge. No matter how degraded the sexual function of woman has become, its vast possibilities for religious knowledge are still present; woman requires only a man who approaches her with his lust purified into love. American woman of the present is still the warm and fertile earth of America, as the reminders of Pocahontas indicate. Thus, this section represents an advance beyond the refusal to know woman's function which we saw in "Southern Cross." We have a bridge which leads from "Southern Cross" to "Virginia"—a bridge within a bridge (if we see that all of "Three Songs" is a bridge between "Cape Hatteras" and the last three sections of the poem).

In the third and last song, "Virginia," vision is still earnestly sought for and applied to the problem of reclaiming the importance of the female principle of mystic America. The title of the song suggests many functions which Crane intended the lyric to fulfill. Just as America was to receive and enclose and finally transfigure all the materialistic endeavors of mankind, so in the figure of the Virgin Mary the full significance of the partial fulfilments and mistakes of Eve and Magdalene takes on spiritual meaning. We are reminded also perhaps that in the vision which followed "the Dance," Pocahontas was celebrated as "virgin to the last of men. . . ." Furthermore, the name of the section recalls the lovely geographical home of the legendary Pocahontas, recalls to us the cartwheeling figure of Powhatan's daughter whom the pioneers saw and the great vision of freedom and beauty which lured the European invaders on westward. Columbus, in "Ave Maria," had prayed for a sign from Mary ("Assure us through thy mantle's ageless blue!"), and the protagonist seems to find a reincarnation of the efficacious and glorious Virgin—a merger of the mother of Christ with Pocahontas—in the lovely office worker ("O blue-eyed Mary with the claret scarf,/Saturday Mary, mine!"). The epithet "Saturday Mary" suggests that religious truth for America may not be found wholly in terms of the old

Hebraic-Christian tradition: American materialism must be absorbed into the new religion. It is true that this poem reveals that the flowers which grew in such wildly charming profusion in the land of the protagonist's quest for Pocahontas and Whitman have been tamed to grow in pots and window boxes, and the protagonist is certainly aware of the material ugliness of the age ("Crap-shooting gangs in Bleecker reign"). But there is beauty in the city, and the image of the lovely maiden gives it a synthesis and focus as useful as that of Pocahontas for a simpler, wilder, and earlier America. The encounter with the image of "Saturday Mary" insures for the protagonist the permanence of the vision of Whitman and the opportunity to search endlessly for the meaning of an America which still lies fresh and virgin though not yet completely understood.

The quest is not ended with "Three Songs"; the full significance of the search for meaning must await the experiences of "Quaker Hill," "The Tunnel," and "Atlantis." However, an important step has been taken in bridging the apparent gap between the mechanical triumphs and the spiritual aridity of twentieth-century life. The vision of Whitman has been sustained in these songs by a kind of dialectic process—from Eve as thesis, through Magdalene as antithesis, to Mary as synthesis. Crane's poem has stressed the position of women all the way through, recalling Whitman's preoccupation with the importance of mothers and wives. The vision of "Cathedral Mary" leads quite naturally into "Quaker Hill," where the protagonist attempts to encounter a new thesis, the tragic view and disappointments of creative women—Emily Dickinson and Isadora Duncan, who, in Crane's view, attempted to resolve the chaos by facing it, just as the protagonist had faced it in earlier sections and must yet face it in "The Tunnel."

Far, then, from marring the structure of *The Bridge*, these three songs provide a bridge between the apparently disparate American worlds of Pocahontas and of Dickinson, Duncan and Hart Crane. Crane felt sure, as did Whitman, that a total vision of America had to include both male and female elements; like the protagonist of "Song of Myself," the protagonist of *The Bridge* had to be a kind of Tiresias figure, and "Three Songs" afforded Crane an opportunity to deal extensively, though in a brief lyrical section, with the question of woman and her potentialities. The early sections of the poem had made clear that evil and sterility resulted from the failure to recognize the spiritual aspects of woman and the love of which she was capable. The songs suggest a way of fusing the experience of the twentieth century with the mystic dream of the discoverers and pioneers and look forward to the achieved vision of "Atlantis." Finally, as I have suggested earlier, these songs provide a desirable lyrical interlude between the grandiose apotheosis of Whitman and the terrible descent into the purgatorial experience of "Quaker Hill" and "The Tunnel." If Crane's critics wish to dismiss "Three Songs" on grounds of taste, one cannot quarrel with them. But to suggest that the three lyrics are inorganic or inappropriately placed with reference to "Cape Hatteras" and "Quaker Hill" is simply to misread *The Bridge* and to obscure Crane's intention and achievement.

L. S. Dembo

The Tragic Argument

Ever since its appearance in 1930, *The Bridge* has been a subject of controversy. Among its detractors are some of the most acute critics of Crane's generation: Yvor Winters, Allen Tate, Richard Blackmur, F. O. Matthiessen, Malcolm Cowley. Although all these critics are willing to concede that Crane was a gifted poet—perhaps even a great poet—none has considered *The Bridge* to be anything but a failure.[1] Indeed, the word "failure" usually appears in any commentary on the poem, whether the writer is pointing out a passage to be admired, praising Crane for his noble but unsuccessful effort, or simply condemning him. The most serious charges are, first, that Crane is not really dealing with meaningful events in American experience as an epic

From *Hart Crane's Sanskrit Charge: A Study of "The Bridge"* (Ithaca, New York: Cornell University Press, 1960), pp. 3–22. Reprinted by permission of the author.
[1] See in particular Blackmur's *Language as Gesture* (New York, 1935) and *The Double Agent* (New York, 1935), Cowley's "A Preface to Hart Crane," *New Republic* 62 (April 23, 1930) and *Exile's Return* (New York, 1951), Matthiessen's "American Poetry, 1920–40," *Sewanee Review* 55 (Jan.–March, 1947), Tate's *Reactionary Essays* (New York, 1936), and Winters' "The Progress of Hart Crane," *Poetry* 36 (June, 1930), *Primitivism and Decadence* (New York, 1937), and *In Defense of Reason* (New York, 1947).

poet should; second, that a loss of faith in his subject which occurred during the writing of the poem destroyed whatever logic there may have been in the original plan; and, finally, that the imagery is generally unfathomable. In short, *The Bridge* has been considered an abortive attempt to establish an American myth and a failure in meaning, form, and style.

These objections have never really been met. I am not sure that anyone has even tried to meet all of them. Those who have treated *The Bridge* sympathetically—for instance, Brom Weber in his critical biography of Crane and Frederick Hoffman in his book on the twenties—make no effort to account for its apparent defects. Yet these objections can be met. *The Bridge* has both meaning and form, neither of which has been appreciated because the kind of experience that the poem presents seems never to have been appreciated. In the matter of style, the problem is merely to understand a number of idiosyncrasies in diction and syntax; Crane is fundamentally not nearly so difficult a poet as Rimbaud or Thomas, for instance.

No one can satisfactorily explain the meaning of *The Bridge* unless he is aware of the particular position from which Crane approached his material. Critics such as Winters have altogether too easily identified Crane with Whitman, but even though these two poets of the American scene are indisputably part of the same tradition, they differ crucially in temperament; and until we can appreciate this difference, we shall have every inclination to view *The Bridge* wrongly as nothing but an unsuccessful attempt to proclaim Whitman's vision in the modern world. This difference becomes apparent when one compares a poem like Whitman's "City of Orgies" with one like Crane's "Possessions," both of which are concerned with urban life.[2] To Whitman, the "orgies, walks and joys," "the interminable rows of houses," "the processions in the streets"—mundane reality, in other words—are all able to be transcended:

> but as I pass O Manhattan, your frequent and swift
> flash of eyes offering me love,

[2] "City of Orgies" appears in *Leaves of Grass,* Rinehart Editions, ed. Sculley Bradley (New York, 1949), p. 107. "Possessions" (p. 82) and all other quotations from Crane's poems are from *The Collected Poems of Hart Crane,* Black and Gold Library ($3.50). By permission of Liveright, Publishers, New York. Copyright (R) 1961, Liveright Publishing Corp. (Since all poems by Whitman or Crane cited by me can be found conveniently in the aforementioned volumes, no further page references will be given.)

> Offering response to my own—these repay me,
> Lovers, continual lovers, only repay me.

Here is how Crane responds to Manhattan:

> I, turning, turning on smoked forking spires,
> The city's stubborn lives, desires.

> Tossed on these horns, [he] who bleeding dies,
> Lacks all but piteous admissions to be spilt
> Upon the page whose blind sum finally burns
> Record of rage and partial appetites.

The "record of rage" becomes the poem:

> The pure possession, the inclusive cloud
> Whose heart is fire shall come,—the white wind raze
> All but bright stones wherein our smiling plays.

Although both these poems clearly have optimistic conclusions, they are conclusions of a widely different kind. Crane's speaker attains a personal "pure possession" by consuming himself with rage and lust. Whitman reasserts his spiritual rapport with the city by what he calls in another poem "the measureless ocean of love" within him.

My point is simply this: both Whitman and Crane may have approached their subject (American society) from a position of isolation, but Crane did not share Whitman's "measureless love," that conception which invariably made it possible for Whitman to assert his identity with the world and engendered all his optimism. "Possessions" is optimistic not because an ideal identity has been attained, but because the poet has achieved some kind of personal redemption within his own isolation.

Identity through love ("Personalism") is, of course, the whole principle underlying Whitman's vision of America. In the 1855 preface to *Leaves of Grass*, he wrote that the role of the poet was to "sing the Song of that divine law of Identity, and of Yourself, consistently with the Divine Law of the Universal . . . to arouse and set flowering in men's and women's hearts . . . endless streams of living, pulsating love and friendship directly from them to myself, now and ever."[3] With this attitude Whitman was prepared to account for any evil he saw as merely apparent,

---

[3] *Leaves of Grass*, ed. Emory Holloway (Garden City, 1957), p. 518 note.

transitory, and subordinate to the single force in the world that was meaningful.

Poems like "Possessions" and "Voyages," in which the poet-voyager reaches a belle isle of the imagination wholly beyond the world, indicate that Crane had strong *symboliste* inclinations—that he was not prepared to compromise his personal vision (the pure possession) with an insensitive society and that he was willing to accept isolation.[4] This strain runs throughout much of his early poetry, and had he never written poems like "Faustus and Helen," "Recitative," or, finally, *The Bridge* itself, the problem of evaluating his work would be much easier than it is. But the fact is that Crane could not accept isolation and that he tried to work out a vision in which a personal notion of Absolute Beauty became effective for the whole of industrial civilization, and the isolated lyricist, preoccupied only with his own imagination, found a role in society as a seer. In other words, Crane faced exactly the same problem that Whitman did, but without Whitman's particular kind of solution. Thus we find him saying: "For unless poetry can absorb the machine, i.e., *acclimatize* it as naturally and casually as trees, cattle, galleons, castles and all other human associations of the past, then poetry has failed in its full contemporary function"[5]

An indication of what Crane meant by "acclimatize" appears in an earlier essay:

> It is my hope to go *through* the combined materials of the poem, using our "real" world somewhat as a spring-board. . . . Such a poem is at least a stab at truth. . . . Its evocation will not be toward decoration or amusement, but rather toward a state of consciousness, an "innocence" (Blake) or absolute beauty. In this condition there may be discoverable under new forms certain spiritual illuminations, shining with a morality essentialized from experience directly. . . . It is as though a poem gave the reader as he left it a single, new *word*, never before spoken and impossible to actually enunciate, but self-evident as an active principle in the reader's consciousness henceforward.[6]

---

[4] Crane read extensively in the *symboliste* poets and even published a translation of Jules Laforgue's "Locutions des Pierrot," a reprint of which may be found in Brom Weber's *Hart Crane: A Biographical and Critical Study* (New York, 1948), p. 388.
[5] "Modern Poetry," reprinted in *Collected Poems,* p. 177.
[6] "General Aims and Theories," reprinted in Philip Horton's *Hart Crane: The Life of an American Poet* (New York, 1937), pp. 326–327.

Crane is speaking here in a characteristically romantic idiom. What he means, I think, is this: an Absolute exists that manifests itself in several forms; if these forms are "apprehended" by the poet through the imagination, which alone can bring on the special "state of consciousness," then they will reveal to him the nature of the Absolute itself ("spiritual illuminations"). The "new word" is the poem in which the poet's experience with the Word is presented to the reader. (Crane uses the term "Word" to represent the Absolute in "Voyages" and throughout *The Bridge*.) As early as "Faustus and Helen" (1923), Crane made it apparent that the "new forms" were the products of the machine age. Finally, we find him saying:

> I am concerned with the future of America, but not because I think that America has any so-called par value as a state or group of people. . . . It is only because I feel persuaded that here are destined to be discovered certain as yet undefined spiritual quantities, perhaps a new hierarchy of faith not to be developed so completely elsewhere.[7]

The "yet undefined spiritual quantities" were to be defined as the Bridge.

The Bridge is not a naïve attempt to set up a national myth based on technology for its own sake, but an account of the exiled poet's quest for a logos in which the Absolute that he has known in his imagination will be made intelligible to the world. As that logos, the Bridge is neither a god nor a myth unto itself; rather it "lends a myth to God," or is the myth by which the Absolute makes itself understood in the modern world: it is the new embodiment of the Word—"Deity's young name"—just as in the "Ave Maria" section, Christ is the old embodiment of the Word to Columbus.

The most convincing evidence that Crane's starting point was the imaginative ideal of the lyricist lies in his creation of another symbol, one that has no resemblance to anything mechanical and yet manages to dominate most of the action in the poem. Crane has told us that Pocahontas represents the body of the continent, but no one who has read "Faustus and Helen" or "Voyages" would be willing to let the matter rest there. Faustus in pursuit of Helen, the voyager in quest of the Belle Isle, where the "lounged goddess" yields the "imaged Word," is, of course, the

---

[7] *Ibid.,* p. 325.

poet in search of the Absolute. Whatever Pocahontas stands for in American experience—the Indian past that holds a legacy for the modern world, the mysterious body of the continent—her final meaning is, again, simply the Platonic Ideal. She is the Lady, whose "crucial sign" Crane had sought in nearly every line of his mature poetry.

As a quest, *The Bridge* is actually a romantic lyric given epic implications. Crane tried to find in the history of American society some evidence that this society was capable of a psychological experience essentially identical with the poet's ecstatic apprehension of the Ideal as Beauty. The narrator in *The Bridge* thus journeys to a mythic Indian past that represents "the childhood of the continent," becomes an Indian himself, and marries Pocahontas in a ritual fire dance. Having thus learned the Word, attained the guerdon of the goddess, he returns to his own time, where, to use Eliot's expression, he is "attacked by the voices of temptation." Although he now sees Pocahontas not as a fertile goddess, but as a sterile prostitute, the poet keeps his faith and concludes the poem with a hymn celebrating the Bridge as a modern embodiment of the Word.

Seen in this light, the poem obviously is affirmative in its final judgment of society. As late as May, 1930, Crane could say: "The poem, as a whole, is, I think, an affirmation of experience, and to that extent is 'positive' rather than 'negative' in the sense that *The Waste Land* is negative."[8] Thus the disillusion presented in the concluding sections in almost every instance gives way to a restatement of faith, one that rises to ecstasy in "Atlantis." The problem is not to explain Crane's disillusion, but to determine the meaning of his reaffirmation, for by such reaffirmation, Crane seems to have reached Whitman's final position without having acquired Whitman's particular vision of life. In other words we may ask, What is the connection between the experience of the lyricist (the pursuit, capture, loss, and recapture of the Lady), which may be wholly free of social meaning, as in "Voyages," and the social experience of the seer, who ecstatically reaffirms a faith in society's ability to comprehend the Absolute? Does Crane's view of society depend entirely on his personal romantic feelings about Beauty? Until this question is answered, we have no way of knowing whether the poem simply interprets social experience in terms which have meaning only in the imaginative realm of the

---

[8] To Waldo Frank, *The Letters of Hart Crane*, ed. Brom Weber (New York, 1952), p. 351.

lyricist or else makes assertions that are relevant to American life in general. An answer is possible, and it not only does much to clarify the meaning of the poem, but goes a long way toward vindicating its form.

In 1920 or 1921, Crane was exposed to Friedrich Nietzsche's theory of tragedy, a theory that eventually provided him with a metaphysical argument with which to meet disillusion, whatever its source, and thus associated him not merely with Whitman, but with the whole tradition of optimism in nineteenth-century romantic literature. Crane is known to have read only *The Birth of Tragedy*, and he seems to have taken from it just the essentials of the view that it presents.[9] Nietzsche declared that tragedy was produced by two impulses in the Greek world: the Apollonian, which represented the art world of dreamland, and the Dionysian, which represented that of intoxication. The Apollonian artist read and unmasked his dreams; he created through meditation and represented man trusting in his own individuality and reason to confront "a world of sorrows." The Dionysian regarded life not rationally, but with awe, and was spurred on by a "narcotic draught"; he represented man surrendering his individuality in order to blend with his fellows in "mysterious Primordial Unity." The imitator of dreams and the artist of ecstasies are reconciled in the tragic poet; "in his Dionysian drunkenness and mystical self-abnegation, lonesome and apart from revelling choruses, he sinks down, and . . . now, through Appollonian dream-inspiration, his own state, *i.e.*, his oneness with the primal source of the universe, reveals itself to him *in a symbolical dream-picture*."[10]

Examined in terms of Nietzsche's classification, Crane's early poetry almost too neatly represents the Apollonian and Dionysian impulses unreconciled. Most of the poems are dream meditations (e.g., "In Shadow," "Echoes," "The Bathers," "A Postscript," "Modern Craft"). When they do not attempt to present merely an aesthetic impression, they make a conscious and rational appraisal of the dream image: since the poet inhabits a "world of sorrows," the ephemeral garden lady turns up dissolute in a cocktail lounge; the "episode of hands," which promises a homo-

[9] How much Crane actually read of Nietzsche or how deeply he read in him is unknown. Nietzsche was much admired in the twenties, and it seems improbable that Crane would not have read Mencken's *The Philosophy of Nietzsche*, which appeared as early as 1908, or George Burman Foster's articles on the philosopher in *The Little Review* in 1917.
[10] *The Birth of Tragedy*, tr. William Haussman, in *The Complete Works of Friedrich Nietzsche*, ed. Oscar Levy, III (Edinburgh, 1909), 28–29.

sexual and spiritual fulfillment, is never realized, as the poet
reveals in a more contemplative mood.[11] Crane finally responded
to Apollonian dejection by "intoxicating his inquiries." In 1922,
he wrote Gorham Munson:

> Did I tell you of that thrilling experience this last winter in the
> dentist's chair when under the influence of aether and *amnesia*
> my mind spiraled to a kind of seventh heaven of consciousness
> and egoistic dance among the seven spheres—and something like
> an objective voice kept saying to me—"You have the higher
> consciousness—you have the higher consciousness. . . ." A happi-
> ness, ecstatic such as I have known only twice in "inspirations"
> came over me.[12]

The apples that intoxicate the painter in "Sunday Morning
Apples" not only make it possible for his paintings to "rival the
spring," but bring to the poet a spring of his own.

In "For the Marriage of Faustus and Helen" (1923), Crane
made his first attempt to reconcile through tragedy Apollonian
dejection with Dionysian ecstasy, and the three parts of the poem
seem to have been arranged according to a clearly Nietzschean
logic. In Part I, Faustus, by evocation, presents a dream picture
of Helen and meditates on the possibility of attaining her. In the
"dance and sensual culmination" of Part II, drunk on the narcotic
of jazz, he surrenders to a grotesque vision of Helen that he never
would have accepted while he was sober. In Part III, he assumes
a tragic role. He has a renewed dream of Helen, but the goddess
is no longer the mere Gioconda of his imagination; she personifies
tragedy itself. "In "unbinding" his throat "of fear and pity,"
Faustus, who has been involved in the World War as an aviator,
purges himself of guilt and with Dionysian laughter gives voice
to the new society. His union with Helen is an Apollonian dream
that presents a picture of his Dionysian oneness with society and
the universe.

Dream, meditation, and ecstasy are the three states in which
the poet interprets American society in *The Bridge*. The distinc-
tions are clearest in the Powhatan's Daughter sequence: thus
"The Harbor Dawn" presents a dream vision of Pocahontas that
vanishes; in "The River," the awakened dreamer makes a rational
appraisal of modern America and tries to find in it the elements

---

[11] I am speaking here of "Episode of Hands" and "The Bridge of Estador."
Although written a year apart (1920 and 1921), these poems deal with a
single experience. They are reprinted in Weber, pp. 384–385.
[12] *Letters*, pp. 91–92.

that will help him recapture the goddess; in the ecstasy of "The Dance" lies the poet's answer to all meditation. In the sections that follow Powhatan's Daughter, the poet indicates that, having returned from the mythic past to the modern world, he can now apprehend the goddess only by extrarational means. Contemplation of the realities of a technological society—war in "Cape Hatteras," the deterioration of love and beauty in "Three Songs," Philistinism in "Quaker Hill," and metropolitan chaos in "The Tunnel"—brings only despair. Yet in nearly every instance, we find the poet reaffirming his faith, either with an ecstatic tone in his voice, as in "Cape Hatteras," with a note of determination not logically justified by the context, as in "Quaker Hill," or with an unrestrained ecstatic hymn, as in the finale.

The justification of this ecstasy—that is, the answer to our original question about the relation of personal awareness of Beauty and social optimism—lies in Crane's broad view of the nature of tragedy. Crane used the expression "the acceptance of tragedy through destruction" to describe the vision in "Faustus and Helen." By "destruction," he meant, first, the psychological destruction of the exiled poet, who, in such poems as "Legend" and "Possessions," spent "himself out again and yet again" in suffering and confusion; and, second, the moral destruction of a poetless and therefore blind society, drawn toward a "mocked confusion/Of apish nightmares into steel-strung stone" ("Key West"). By "the acceptance of tragedy," Crane meant a willingness to believe in what Nietzsche called the eternal life that "exists beyond all phenomena, and in spite of all annihilation." Simply put, Crane accepted the proposition that resurrection always follows suffering and death. That is really the essence of what he took from Nietzsche. Having spent himself out, the poet attained the "bright logic" (the Word) that "strings some constant harmony." In "Recitative," the experience is made public: the poet returns to the ruined world of men to recite the Word (the crucial sign) that will bring redemption.

Tragedy made the poet's biography and social history analogues of one another. The poet is qualified to be a seer because his own cycle of suffering, destruction, and redemption is a mirror of the death and rebirth of civilizations through war and decay ("Faustus and Helen"). In accepting his crucial sign, society listens to its own imagination and moves beyond tragedy to resurrection; its breath is released, its throat unbound of fear and pity. Thus: "The imagination spans beyond despair,/Out-pacing bargain, vocable and prayer." In Shelley's world, the poet alone fell upon the thorns of life and bled; in Crane's, the act had universal implications:

> Lift up . . .
>   Thy face
> From charred and riven stakes, O
> Dionysus, Thy
> Unmangled target smile. ["Lachrymae Christi"]

By 1926, when Crane began working on *The Bridge* in earnest, he had already formulated in half a dozen poems (and he was not a prolific writer) a vision of experience in which destruction—whatever its form, in whatever area it occurred—became the medium by which a "positive goal" was attained. The poet dreams, meditates on the lack of substance of all dreams, and suffers. Yet in the tragic view, such Apollonian dejection is merely part of a larger Dionysian process. The imagination always spans beyond despair; beyond suffering lies illumination; beyond chaos, social regeneration; beyond dismemberment, reintegration. As the epigraph to *The Bridge* suggests, the poet is a Job, whose faith must withstand the test of a "cruel Inquisitor" ("Ave Maria"); the epigraph to "The Tunnel" (taken from Blake) implies that he must pass "Right thro' the Gates of Wrath" to "Find the Western Path."

Crane did not lose faith in his myth—that is, in the manifestation of the Absolute in the modern world. It was neither the Word nor its manifestations that he doubted, but ability of the poet to communicate the Word and of society to accept it. As Crane has interpreted it in *The Bridge,* tragedy prophesies; it does not describe. (The Bridge is a "Terrific threshold of the prophet's pledge.") Its proposition is that society holds within it the possibility of its own redemption, not that it has already been redeemed. The technology that has produced the subway and what it stands for can also produce the Bridge, but modern man will stay on the subway until the poet leads him to the Bridge, speaks the Word that holds his vision of the Absolute. Society will be redeemed when it understands its tragic nature and through its imagination, which speaks through the poet, moves beyond tragedy to a knowledge of divinity. *The Bridge* ends in a question mark, not an exclamation point, just as Crane's first mature poem is entitled "For the Marriage . . ." and not simply "The Marriage of Faustus and Helen." The tragic argument provided Crane with a "metaphysical comfort," as Nietzsche said it did the Greeks, but Crane was willing to take comfort in possibilities. And the reason he was willing to do so is that, whether the poet succeeded or failed, he at least achieved in this scheme a heroic stature. In the constant questioning of faith that the narrator must endure throughout the last sections, there is a vague suggestion of Nietzsche's theory of "eternal recurrence" (that the hero or superman must realize that all his struggles will be in vain and that, in an endless series of lives, he will have to endure them again and again). But what is important is that the tragic principle invests his struggles with dignity and justifies his "Yea-saying" to life even when he is faced with failure in communicating the Word. It seems to me that, whatever his declared intentions, Crane's real purpose in writing *The Bridge* was to create an environment in which the poet was able to transcend the impotent-clown image that was his only face in a nontragic, nonheroic world. Only in a blind but redeemable society—a society in which tragedy was possible—could the poet acquire what Crane thought a befitting role.

I have suggested that far from being an eccentric innovator, on the one hand, or merely a Whitman *manqué*, on the other, Crane belongs to a tradition of nineteenth-century optimism, the whole impulse of which was to establish the role of the visonary and to provide a supernatural answer to moral chaos and to suffering.[13] Indeed, one can go so far as to say that in this sense Crane is as closely related to Emerson, the chief spokesman of American optimism, as he is to Whitman. For instance, in the prefatory poem to "Experience" we find Emerson writing:

> The lords of life, the lords of life,—
> I saw them pass,
> In their own guise,
> Like and unlike,
> Portly and grim. . . .
> Little man, least of all,

---

[13] For a discussion of this theme in American literature in general, see Henry Myers, *Tragedy: A View of Life* (Ithaca, 1956). In his treatment of Whitman, Myers distinguishes between "optimistic" and "tragic" as follows: "Optimism cannot mean other than [the belief] that the amount of good in the world outweighs the amount of evil"; one who holds the tragic attitude (Whitman, for example) believes that "good and evil are both necessary aspects of experience, that one implies the other, and that the qualities of both . . . remain in a state of balance" (p. 88). I have not held to this distinction in my argument; by "optimism" I mean simply the belief that one can come to terms with or transcend "evil" in whatever shape it manifests itself; in this sense, the tragic attitude is merely a form of optimism.

> Among the legs of his guardians tall,
> Walked about with puzzled look. . . .
> Dearest Nature, strong and kind,
> Whispered, "Darling, never mind!
> To-morrow they will wear another face,
> The founder thou! these are thy race!"[14]

As Nature's darling, it is the poet-child who will not only inherit, but redeem the world, for he has the visionary eye that sees harmony beyond chaos,

> eyes,
> Which chose, like meteors, their way,
> And rived the dark with private ray. . . .
> Through man, and woman, and sea, and star
> Saw the dance of nature forward far;
> Through worlds, and races, and terms, and times
> Saw musical order, and pairing rhymes.[15]

Even though Emerson does not have the same emotional intensity as either Whitman or Crane, poems like "Bacchus" reveal that the ecstatic element was important in his thinking. In his essay on the poet, for instance, he writes: "If a man is inflamed and carried away by his thought, to that degree that he forgets the authors and the public and heeds only this one dream which holds him like an insanity, let me read his paper, and you may have all the arguments and histories and criticism."[16] The "musical perfection" that lay "underneath the inharmonious and trivial particulars" was, indeed, Pocahontas lying beneath the "wires, whistles, and steam" of twentieth-century America. "The ideal shall be real to thee, and the impressions of the actual world shall fall like summer rain, copious, but not troublesome to thy invulnerable essence."[17] The Bridge lay beyond the Tunnel: "But in the darkest, meanest things/There alway, alway something sings."[18] And the poet writing history was the poet writing about himself: "All public facts are to be individualized, all private facts are to be generalized. Then at once History becomes fluid and true, and Biography deep and sublime."[19]

---

[14] *Essays, Second Series,* in *The Complete Works of Ralph Waldo Emerson,* III (Boston, 1903), 43.
[15] Prefatory poem to "The Poet," *ibid.,* p. 1.
[16] *Op. cit.,* p. 32.
[17] *Ibid.,* p. 42.
[18] "Music," in *Poems, Complete Works,* IX, 365.
[19] "History," in *Essays, First Series, Complete Works,* II, 21.

I do not mean to suggest that Emerson was a model for Crane; in fact, there is no evidence that Crane even read him deeply. My point is that Crane's attempt to find a visionary solution to those elements in experience that would alienate the imagination makes him traditionally romantic in a definable way. It is not that he shared Emerson's belief in the Over-Soul or Whitman's in Personalism, and he certainly reveals no interest in Nietzsche's Will to Power—his "Superman" is simply the visionary, no more, no less; what he does share with his predecessors is the tragic conception implied in their beliefs. Crane was not really trying to celebrate some transcendental force in the world—his ideal is unspecified and goes by no name other than the Word or Beauty. But for his purposes, a vague ideal was sufficient, and his purposes were, as I have suggested, to invest the poet and his world with tragic dignity; only in such dignity could Crane find the meaning in life that he sought, and for a man who came of age in the twenties, that was being metaphysical enough.

John Unterecker

The Architecture of *The Bridge*

Perhaps our principal difficulty in appreciating *The Bridge* as a work of art is that we read it too carefully. It is a long poem and, for most readers, a difficult one. Somewhere along the way, most of us, I suspect, get bogged down in a passage that seems to demand concentrated work. Good explicators that we are, we stop to work on it.

Such explication is, needless to say, ultimately necessary. And in the course of these remarks I want to suggest certain kinds of explicatory approaches which seem to me most fruitful. The poem is a good one and it can stand all the careful readings we can bring to it. Yet if we start with explication, we may never get around to reading the poem straight through—end to end—without interruption.

I am convinced, however, that if we do read it straight through, a good many of our difficulties will disappear. What looks like fragmentation and downright disorganization is likely in an uninterrupted reading to fall together into coherence. Because they will pass by rapidly enough for us to remember them, we will

From John Unterecker, "The Architecture of *The Bridge.*" *Wisconsin Studies in Contemporary Literature,* Volume III, Number 2 (© 1962 by the Regents of the University of Wisconsin), pp. 5-20.

either notice or at least properly be affected by the dozens and dozens of linking devices that Crane carefully put into his work to hold the individual and very different sections together.

The sections do, of course, appear disorganized. Yet precisely in the appearance of disorganization—the seeming unrelatedness of section to section—may be something very close to the basic form of the work. I am not trying here to be ingenious. I am simply trying to describe what I think Crane himself regarded as an important form in the tradition in which he was working.

Perhaps if I name a few works in that tradition, I can suggest a little more accurately what I think Crane was doing in organizing *The Bridge* as he did.

Some writers of his tradition are, in fact, referred to in *The Bridge:* particularly Blake, Melville, and Whitman. To these, I think, we should add T. S. Eliot, Ezra Pound, and James Joyce. There are others, but these at least suggest a pattern that Crane fits into.

Blake, Melville, Whitman, Eliot, Pound, and Joyce. At first they look like strange bedfellows; but if one lines up Blake's prophetic books, *Moby Dick*, Whitman's "Passage to India," *Ulysses*, the Mauberley poems, and "The Waste Land", certain structural similarities all but leap at one. For one thing, each of these works has a mosaic structure. Each is compounded from a number of what at first look like almost completely independent sections. And in most of these works, the authors have gone to some trouble to make the sections as different as possible.

One has only to recollect the jolting experience of a first reading of *Moby Dick* to see what I mean: the shock of bouncing from that enormous collection of epigraphs, the "extracts," to the simple narrative of the opening chapters, to the considerably more complex narrative that follows—a narrative broken by direct address to the reader, reported dreams, and intrusive low-level symbolic imagery—to annotated catalogues of whales, to such set pieces of dense symbolism as the chapter on "The Whiteness of the Whale," and finally to "The Chase" itself which, if one's reading has been lucky, pulls the whole work together.

Similarly, the "form" of *Ulysses* involves as many different forms as there are chapters. And the sections of the Mauberley poems and those of "The Waste Land," are radically different one from the other. Even in Blake and in Whitman, where there seems to be a little more continuity of technique, one's first reaction is an awareness of the disjointedness of things.

The reader always, of course, in any successful work puts the pieces together; but in works of the sort I have listed, he knows that he is doing it. He is constantly being reminded—by the form itself—that the whole work is made up of a series of parts. And he is also constantly being reminded that the structure the author is working on is not going to be finished until the reader has finished the last page. When he gets to that last page, the reader, if the work is successful, ought to have a feeling of congruence. The large sections that have seemed independent will be discovered to be bolted together into a substantial unit that will be remembered as *Ulysses* or *Moby Dick* or even as *The Bridge*.

We are, I think, best adjusted to forms of this sort in the other arts—particularly in music and in painting, where the element of "composition" is accepted to be at the heart of the work. One has only to think, for instance, of the water colors of such a painter as William Sommer or John Marin, both of whom Crane greatly admired, to find analogous structures—great blocks of color held together by the echoing pattern of a superimposed linking design.

What the writer gains from a structure of this sort is, of course, the advantage of shifted ground. All of the sections point in toward one center and are, needless to say, linked by it; but as we move from section to section in reading the work, perspectives change and we see the subject the writer is working on from new and illuminating angles. (Some readers, who like always to see things only from one point of view, find such shifts disconcerting. Disliking catalogues, they object to catalogues in Whitman—who sometimes uses them very deftly indeed. Bored by catechisms, they find dull the questions and answers of the Ithaca section of *Ulysses*. Or, able to use information only if it is pleasantly disguised in plot, they criticize Melville for his spectacularly intrusive sections of whaling facts. Readers of this kind, needless to say, find the superficial fragmentation of such a work as *The Bridge* upsetting. Incapable of liking all of its parts, they label it a failure—sometimes a brilliant one.)

Crane certainly exploits all of the possibilities of superficial fragmentation. He moves backwards and forwards in time, he shifts suddenly from third person, to first, to second, and back again to third; he examines the bridge he is constructing from above and below, from north, south, east, and west; he employs diction that ranges from advertising jargon and slang on the one hand to lyrical elegance on the other; he shifts tone rapidly, drawing, among a good many others, on elegiac, satirical, and even sentimental attitudes.

Gradually, as he circles his subject, letting us see it from as many angles as we can, his bridge emerges. Hinting his technique in the epigraph from *The Book of Job*—"From going to and fro in the earth, and from walking up and down in it"—he leads us up and down, in and out, to and fro until we have built, as he intended, his bridge in ourselves. Like the motion picture audience of the "Proem"—"multitudes bent toward some flashing scene"—we construct from the flashed separate frames of the sections something "never disclosed" in any one of them.

I labor this point about the total organization of the poem because all too often *The Bridge* is criticized as if it were a volume of unrelated or at best loosely-related lyrics. The "Indiana" subsection is a favorite target of such criticism. By itself, of course, "Indiana" is as sentimental as it is accused of being. And if it were an independent personal lyric, which it is not, it would certainly merit the attack. Yet in context, it very neatly opposes the whirlwind of "The Dance" and both anticipates the subject matter of "Cutty Sark" and acts as a foil to its jazz rhythms.

In spite of its radically different sections, the poem is remarkably coherent, the sections being locked together in all sorts of ways; and some, at least, of its integrating devices have clear associations with other works in the tradition that I have been discussing.

The "plot" of the poem, for example, sounds almost like a digest of Joyce's *Ulysses*. A young man awakens in the early dawn, gazes out over harbor and city, spends a day wandering through the streets of his metropolis, gradually becoming involved in its corruption, and, after agonizing disillusionment and drunkenness—a kind of spiritual descent to Hades—comes, at the very end of the poem, in the pre-dawn hours of the next morning, to an illuminating vision of order in which he can accept himself and his world.

During his wanderings in his city, its sights and sounds trigger memories both of his own youth and of the youth of his country, its history and its mythology.

Like Joyce's young man, Crane's young man is also concerned with the writers and artists who have significantly shaped his world. Americans—Whitman, Poe, Melville, Emily Dickinson, and Isadora Duncan—rub shoulders with Plato, Seneca, Marlowe, Shakespeare, Milton, and Hopkins.

If plot and a good deal of the organization seem to hint of a careful reading of Joyce—and we know, of course, that Crane not only read *Ulysses* but that he even went so far as to prepare a gloss of parts of it, a gloss which he copied out with passages from the text for a friend who had not yet seen a copy—both the notion of an American myth and much of its machinery come from Whitman, particularly Whitman's "Passage to India" and "Crossing Brooklyn Ferry," though Crane also paraphrases or quotes very, very widely from other works by Whitman in the course of his poem.

But the Whitman influence, though real, works most directly into the poem by way of contemporary admirers of Whitman, particularly Waldo Frank and William Carlos Williams. Frank, in letters to and in conversations with Crane, insisted on the primacy of Whitman's view of American life. It was Williams, however, who in poetry that could accurately be described as Whitmanesque and in his prose study *In the American Grain*, gave Crane material that was immediately useful. For not only did Crane take the epigraph to "Powhatan's Daughter" from *In the American Grain*, he also, as he acknowledged in a now-lost letter to Williams, drew on the thesis of *American Grain* for much of the "argument" of *The Bridge* and on Williams' early poem "The Wanderer" for a good deal of the imagistic structure. Even without that letter (it was destroyed by Dr. Williams' overly-zealous, neat maid), the reader of "The Wanderer" should have no difficulty in identifying material that Crane adapted to his own needs.

Published in 1917 as the final poem in Williams' *A Book of Poems, Al Que Quiere!*, "The Wanderer" developed in seven sections an account of the still-vital power of a symbolic feminine force. In "Advent," the opening section, she puts to a young poet "crossing the ferry/ With the great towers of Manhattan" before him, a question that anticipates neatly the crucial question that runs not only beneath *The Bridge* but as well beneath all of Crane's work: " How shall I be a mirror to this modernity?" The young poet sees her much as Crane sees his Pocahontas figure: "She sprang from the nest, a young crow,/ Whose first flight circled the forest." Later she reappears to him as a swimmer in the Manhattan-enclosing river and at the end of the first section as a sea gull rising above it, "vanishing with a wild cry." She becomes for Williams' young poet a figure representing the total past of the country "In whom age in age is united—/ Indifferent, out of sequence, marvelously!" He sees her "attiring herself" before him, "Taking shape before me for worship,/ A red leaf that falls upon a stone!" And though in modern times she may possess no longer her one-time forest grace, she is still remarkably potent: "At her throat is loose gold, a single chain/ From among many." Like the figures of Crane's poem, she is to be found where river and land meet: "Toward the river! Is it she there?" And like Crane's spirit-of-the-land-fallen-on-evil-days, the corrupt women of "Southern Cross" and "National Winter Garden," Williams' woman in the "Broadway" section is reduced to a harlot, "After the youth of all cities" but from whom still can come release as the poet calls for "A new grip upon those garments that brushed me/ In days gone by on beach, lawn, and in forest!/ May I be lifted still, up and out of terror,/ Up from before the death living around me—."

If, like Crane later, Williams associated his female spirit of the land with water, he also associated his male figure with wind. Like Crane's Maquokeeta, Williams' masculine figure is revealed toward the end of "The Wanderer" in the "Soothsay" section to be "the wind coming that stills birds," and is addressed directly in a prophetic apostrophe almost precisely parallel to Crane's vision of the whirlwind:

> The din and bellow of the male wind
> Leap then from forest into foam!
> Lash about from low into high flames . . .

Finally the poet is led to the river itself, where the ancient female, now both mother and mistress, insists on his identification with it also: "Enter, youth, into this bulk!/ Enter, river, into this young man!" He experiences it completely—both "the crystal beginning of its days" and the "utter depth of its rottenness."

Crane's reliance on Williams' poem is, I think, obvious, just as is his reliance on Joyce's novel. I do not, however, mean to suggest that he imitated either. As every writer borrows, he borrowed; but his borrowings are inevitably woven into a poem uniquely his own. Second-hand themes and images are nothing new in literature. What Crane found in these writers and in a good many others was material that could be adapted to the mythic structure that he was creating. *The Bridge* as a mythic structure has, however, been very fully and very recently discussed by L. S. Dembo in his book *Hart Crane's Sanskrit Charge* and, except for these observations on Joyce and Williams, all I could say on that subject would be no more than marginalia to Mr. Dembo's very thorough study.

Not quite so much attention, however, has been paid to the very careful way in which section of *The Bridge* is linked to section and the equally ingenious way in which the temporal and spatial schemes of the poem are integrated.[1]

One of Crane's favorite devices is simple verbal repetition. A phrase or word will be picked up in one section and reworked in the next, almost always in a completely different context. It is exactly this sort of repetition which binds the lyrical "Proem" entitled "To Brooklyn Bridge" to the following "Ave Maria" section, a dramatic monologue by Columbus as he approaches Europe on his return voyage from America.

Crane set up in his "Proem" a great deal of the imagery he will draw on throughout his poem—the Brooklyn Bridge itself (his core image), the air over it patterned by a circling gull and above that gull a blazing sun, the river which flows under the bridge, the two shores, and the underworld counterpart of the bridge, the subway which cuts below the river.

The particular link, however, that most firmly joins "Proem" to "Ave Maria" comes in the last stanza of the "Proem," a direct address to the bridge:

> O Sleepless as the river under thee,
> Vaulting the sea, the prairies' dreaming sod,
> Unto us lowliest sometime sweep, descend
> And of the curveship lend a myth to God.

The bridge, as Crane has indicated earlier in the "Proem," is sleepless because always simultaneously active and passive. Though fixed, it is an image of freedom. The "traffic lights," for instance, that "skim" its surface in constant motion, like the stars moving across the fixed bridge of the sky, "condense eternity" by giving us a way of apprehending a still form filled with motion. The bridge itself, as he says, is an unmoving "stride" across the river, yet an unmoving stride which contains "some motion ever unspent."

This paradox of the still form compounded from motion produces the bridge, held in place by the active conflict between its lifting cables and its dragging span, "stayed" by its freedom, and

---

[1] Perhaps the strongest discussion of the imagistic structure of *The Bridge* is in Sister M. Bernetta Quinn's *The Metamorphic Tradition in Modern Poetry* (New Brunswick, N. J., 1955).

imitated by the seagull above it which moves in an "inviolate curve" and which builds above the bridge, "over the *chained* bay waters," "Liberty."*

The sleepless bridge is linked therefore to river and sea—also sleepless (always in motion and always contained by shores) and like the bridge both *free* and *chained*—and is opposed to the "dreaming sod" of land. And Crane's plea at the end of the "Proem" is that, unlike the gull above it which curves out of sight, the sleepless bridge will descend "and of the curveship lend a myth to God"—give God a shape contemporary humans can deal with—for God is also ideally both bridge and perfect curve, the chastiser and protector who once had made a covenant with man in the shape of a rainbow.

All of this material and a good deal more finds an echo in the first main division of the poem, Columbus' "Ave Maria" as he "gazes toward Spain." The bridge itself is echoed, as Columbus' invoked God is praised for his omnipresence, his "teeming span" which bridges the distance between Ganges and Spain. The form of the double uprights of the suspension bridge is echoed in the "poles" of the ship and even in the waves themselves—"the sea's green crying towers"—the trough of the waves forming one more of those curves which from this point on dominate the poem. The circling seagull that had made an "inviolate curve" above the curve of the bridge is echoed as Columbus recollects the natives who "came out to us crying/ 'The Great White Birds' "; and the "white rings of tumult" that the gull had made in the "Proem" are echoed in Columbus' vision of a round earth—his sailing eyes finally having "accreted," "enclosed,"

> This turning rondure whole, this crescent ring
> Sun-cusped and zoned with modulated fire
> Like pearls that whisper through the Doge's hands.

Similarly, above the round earth that Columbus thought he had circled lies the circle of the heavens and the stars, the "sapphire wheel" of the night, where, again circling, God's "once whirling feet" had one-time raced. God himself is seen here as circle within circle, the "white toil of heaven's cordons" who musters "in holy rings" all sails on earth—those of gull and those of ship. And on God's brows is set—one last circle—a crown, "the kindled Crown"

---

* Unless otherwise noted, all italics in passages quoted from Crane are mine.

beneath the cruel, loving flames of which "meridians reel" God's purpose.

But unlike the bridge Crane had evoked in the "Proem"—"O Sleepless as the river under thee," the sleepless bridge which was of its curveship to "lend a myth to God"—Columbus' God is "apart" and is invoked in terms of a *sleeping* consciousness, both distant from yet acting on man. "O Thou who *sleepest* on Thyself," he is addressed. And the passage goes on to recapitulate by-now-familiar imagery:

> O Thou who sleepest on Thyself, apart
> Like ocean athwart lanes of death and birth,
> And all the eddying breath between dost search
> Cruelly with love thy parable of man,—
> Inquisitor! incognizable Word
> Of Eden and the enchained Sepulchre,
> Into thy steep savannahs, burning blue,
> Utter to loneliness the sail is true.

The sleepless bridge is therefore a myth for God, and man is sleeping God's parable. Like the bridge, God is himself both free and bound—the abstract free Word but as well the enchained mundane Sepulchre.

The joints between the first and second large sections—the watery "Ave Maria" and the continental "Powhatan's Daughter" —are if possible even more numerous, largely because "Powhatan's Daughter" is so very long and is broken into subsections. But the joints which please me most come precisely at the end of "Ave Maria" and at the very beginning of "Powhatan's Daughter" —in fact, within the epigraph; and they are, in a way, almost outlandishly unlikely, for they connect the awful fiery God of Columbus' vision with the twelve-year-old girl who was the flesh, not the myth, of Pocahontas. (It is worth observing in passing, incidentally, that it is Crane's habit always to begin with the simplest level of any image that is going eventually to be destined for symbolic extension. Though before he is finished, almost everything in his poem will be bridge or bridging, all of the bridges are keyed closely to the real Brooklyn Bridge with which the poem begins. Similarly, though Pocahontas is to become symbolic of the red clay of the American soil, she appears in Crane's first reference to her as an altogether physical "wanton" child.)

The God Columbus invoked in his section had been seen in terms of the "once whirling feet" that had swept through the heavens and that were associated with the "sapphire wheel" of

stars. He had been an unforgettable God of thunder and lightning
(Columbus insists: "Elohim, still I hear thy sounding heel"), and
his manifestations continue to strike terror "naked in the/ trem-
bling heart" through the power of his still potent "Hand of Fire."

All of this imagery—wheel, whirling feet, heel, and naked illumination—is reduced in the epigraph of "Powhatan's Daughter" to
entirely human terms:

> "—Pocahuntus, a well-featured but wanton yong girle . . . of the
> age of eleven or twelve years, get the boyes forth with her into
> the market place, and make them *wheele*, falling on their *hands*,
> turning their *heels* upwards, whom she would followe, and *wheele*
> so herself, *naked* as she was, all the fort over."

The sapphire wheel becomes here the wheeling children, the whirling feet and Hand of Fire of God becomes the hands and feet of
cartwheeling seventeenth-century juvenile delinquents and the
naked terror that God inspires becomes a naked "wanton yong
girle."

Within "Powhatan's Daughter" unobtrusive joints of the same
kind hold subsection to subsection—unobtrusive because the second appearance is almost always in a context completely different
from the first. One really has to do a little looking to see such
links. It is easy enough, for example, to notice dream in "Harbor
Dawn," the first subsection of "Powhatan's Daughter," because
the subject matter is itself an awakening from sleep. With dawn
comes "a tide of voices" "midway in your dream." But only the
perceptive reader notes consciously that all the subsequent material in the remaining parts of "Powhatan's Daughter" is dream
material—a dream of the continental past that gives us a history
and a myth to balance Columbus' seagoing freight from Europe.
Yet Crane almost leans over backwards to insist on the dream-
center of this very large division of his poem. Dreams interweave
all through "Van Winkle" and into "The River" which explicitly
"spends your dream," a dream that earlier in that section had
been assembled by the "keen instruments" of telegraph and tele-
phone which, "strung to a vast precision/Bind town to town and
dream to ticking dream." The whirlwind manifestation of Maquokeeta in "The Dance" is really nothing more nor less than dream-
vision. And, again explicitly, in "Indiana," Crane tells us in no
uncertain terms that the Indian dream is very much ending
("Bison thunder rends my *dreams* no more"), that it is ending
—as it should—with the last subsection of the dream-oriented
"Powhatan's Daughter" section:

> The morning-glory, climbing the morning long
> Over the lintel on its wiry vine,
> Closes before the dusk, furls in its song
> As I close mine . . .

If the dream of the Indian past binds together all five subsections of "Powhatan's Daughter," other links tie individual subsections one to the other. The last word of "Harbor Dawn," for example, *sleep*, is echoed almost immediately in the opening of the "Van Winkle" section: " 'Is this *Sleepy* Hollow, friend?' " And the last three lines of the "Van Winkle" section:

> Keep hold of that nickel for car-change, Rip,—
> Have you got your *"Times"*—?
> And hurry along, Van Winkle—it's getting late!*

anticipate the rush of the express train that opens "The River" section, Rip's nickel subway ride expanding to a trip on "The EXpress," the 20th Century Limited which hurtles across the continent; the plea that he "hurry along . . . it's getting late" expanding to a whole crescendo of motion: "whistling down the tracks/a headlight rushing," "windows flashing roar," "Breathtaking," "so/whizzed the Limited—roared by"; and that New York *Times* that Rip clutches expanding into modern event-making journalism: "an EXpress makes time," the capitalized EX of *EXpress* emphasizing the newspaper pun, the ex-press which in the modern world not only records but actually "makes" time.

All of the examples of linking material that I have been so far concerned with are simple enough for quite casual explication. Much more complicated—so complicated that I can only hint at some of their relationships—are the sorts of links which bind the two principal subsections of "Powhatan's Daughter," "The River" and "The Dance," for within these sections is the first full development of a pair of symbols Crane has from the beginning of the poem been preparing us for. I mean, of course, the serpent of time and the eagle of space.

Crane reaches his first explicit reference to these symbols in a very witty passage which immediately follows his reconstruction of the whizzing express and those hoboes who, "dotting immensity," experience America along the express tracks. Suddenly

---

* Crane's italics.

confessional in the midst of a very elegant rhetorical passage—
a literary device he almost certainly adapted from Whitman—
Crane insists:

> . . . I have trod the rumorous midnights, too,
>
> And past the circuit of the lamp's thin flame
> (O Nights that brought me to her body bare!)
> Have dreamed beyond the print that bound her name.
> Trains sounding the long blizzards out—I heard
> Wail into distances I knew were hers.
> Papooses crying on the wind's long mane
> Screamed redskin dynasties that fled the brain,
> —Dead echoes! But I knew her body there,
> Time like a serpent down her shoulder, dark,
> And space, an eaglet's wing, laid on her hair.

Perhaps that thinly veiled attack on the newspapers—"the print
that bound her name"—is close enough to Rip's *"Times"* and the
"EXpress" pun to be obvious to most readers, but it takes a real
railroad buff to realize that the "papooses crying on the winds
long mane" who "screamed redskin dynasties that fled the brain"
and who are now nothing more than "dead echoes" are in fact
pullman cars whipping along after the express and named after
Indian tribes—our last "literary" link with the Indian.

Both funny and serious, the crying papooses are most valuable
in letting Crane introduce his image of serpent time and eagle
space.

The timely serpent itself is, needless to say, involved in all of
the river references of the poem—the river that flows under the
Brooklyn Bridge, the Mississippi which is the explicit subject of
this "river" section, and all the "streams" and "RUNning brooks"
with which the section abounds. (Those "RUNning brooks," more
ingenious even than the crying papooses of the Pullman, are perhaps worth a digression. Like the papooses, they are also part of
the modern streamliner, cropping up at the end of its violent
passage across the landscape. Crane works into them in a whirlwind of capital letters:

>   . . . WE HAVE THE NORTHPOLE
> WALLSTREET AND VIRGINBIRTH WITHOUT STONES OR
> WIRES OR EVEN RUNning brooks connecting ears
> and no more sermons windows flashing roar
> breathtaking—as you like it . . . eh?

"Connecting," as Crane tells us to, we join sermons to stones and stones to running brooks to come up with the crucial images from Duke Senior's speech on the sweet uses of adversity:

> . . . this our life exempt from public haunt
> Finds tongues in trees, books in the running brooks,
> Sermons in stones and good in everything.

Crane, needless to say, has identified it: "as you like it . . . eh?" But running brooks are one aspect only of the serpent of time.)

Just as all of the river and stream imagery is associated with time and with the serpent, so too is all of the other winding imagery of the poem: the trains, the subways, the telegraph wires, the sea-lanes, the gold trail, the canyons and labyrinths and burrows, the Open Road. Eve's serpent is explicitly associated with it, as are the "stinging coils" of Medusa-Eve's hair, and the "silly snake rings" that mount the strip-tease Magdalene of "National Winter Garden." It is part of the "worm's eye" view that Crane warns us in "Quaker Hill" we shall have to take before we are to find salvation. And finally it comes most fully into its own in "The Tunnel," the serpent's own territory. Only at the very end of the poem, in "Atlantis," do we escape its "labyrinthine mouths of history" and ascend from "Time's realm" upward out of time.

One could, similarly, locate all of the strategically-placed bird associations of eagle-space—from circling gulls that begin the poem to "seagulls stung with rime" that end it, from the whirlwind "Dance" subsection in which the imagery is given its first really extensive development to the "Cape Hatteras" section (the aboveground counterpart of "The Tunnel") which is built around a central imagery of airplanes and open air. Suffice to say, almost every serpent figure is balanced somewhere by a bird.

But time and space, as Crane recognized, though antithetical are interdependent. And it is appropriate therefore that he joins them always following each separate treatment. "The River" glides serpent-like down the length of the continent and its section gives way to "The Dance," a cyclone "swooping in eagle feathers" through the sky. But the more the cyclonic Maquokeeta dances, the more he acquires snake-like characteristics until finally he is recognized in transformation: "Dance, Maquokeeta! snake that lives before,/ That casts his pelt and lives beyond!" The narrator both recognizes the transformation—"I saw thy change begun!"—and participates in it in something approaching total identification, finding within himself as within Maquokeeta "pure serpent, Time itself." However, even this sort of imagery—one of transformation—is not adequate for the design Crane planned, and in the end of the paired "River"-"Dance" subsections, serpent and eagle, time and space, are interwoven: "The serpent with the eagle in the boughs."

Imagistic links of this sort bind section to section and can be found functioning brilliantly in even the most minor divisions of the poem.

Other devices, however, are quite as important in giving *The Bridge* an extraordinary coherence.

I have already mentioned the temporal scheme—the twenty-four-hour action of the plot. This same chronological pattern recurs in each of the major divisions, though it is not always stressed. The "Proem," for example, opens with a reference to dawn ("How many dawns, chill from his rippling rest"), at dead center ticks off noon ("Down Wall, from girder into street noon leaks"), goes on through the afternoon ("All afternoon the cloud-flown derricks turn"), and ends in deep night after the "traffic lights" that "skim" the surface of the bridge in early evening have been stilled ("Under thy shadow by the piers I waited;/Only in darkness is thy shadow clear").

This is only one, however, of a number of temporal patterns that can be recognized in the poem. Crane insists that "some men . . . count . . ./ The river's minute by the far brook's year." And his poem is organized as carefully along a January to January scheme as it is along a dawn to dawn one.

The "Proem" opens almost precisely on January 1: "Already snow submerges an iron year," Crane tells us; and if that doesn't give us the date, he lets us know for more than Christmas is over —for "the City's fiery parcels" are "all undone." We are still in cold weather through the snow storm of "Harbor Dawn"; but by the time we reach "Van Winkle," springtime imagery—like Crane's mother's smile—begins to flicker "through the snow screen." "Cape Hatteras," the center of the poem and a section which in itself contains reference to all four seasons, is dominated by Walt Whitman, the Open Road, and a riotous, airy summer. But it is not until we reach "Quaker Hill," the sixth section of the eight which constitute *The Bridge*, the three-quarter mark, that autumn imagery can come into its own. In "Quaker Hill," however, it runs rampant—from the second epigraph, Emily Dickinson's lines on the autumn, "The gentian weaves her fringes,/ The maple's loom is red," to the last lines of the section, "Leaf after autumnal leaf/ break off,/ descend—/descend—." And when we do descend and enter the seventh section and "The Tunnel," we have already returned to winter, "preparing penguin flexions of the arms" to ward off the "brisk" chill of an early December night which finally drives us into that subway which "yawns the quickest promise home." "Atlantis," the last section, brings us completely round again to our frosty beginning, its imagery all whiteness, its bridge rising in cold shining elegance from black night into the faint azure of a frozen dawn.

Larger still than this temporal division is one in which America's varied pasts are recapitulated, each of the first four major sections investigating one of them: the European heritage in "Ave Maria," the primitive past of the continent in "Powhatan's Daughters," the past of whaling days and exploration in "Cutty Sark," and the nineteenth-century democratic past of Whitman's Open Road in "Cape Hatteras." Splitting past from present, the middle of the poem brings us to those years of the modern celebrated by Whitman; and the last four sections—"Three Songs," "Quaker Hill," "The Tunnel," and "Atlantis"—are devoted to our own time, its corruption of love the subject of "Three Songs," its corruption of friendship and commerce the subject of "Quaker Hill," and its corruption of art a principal subject of "The Tunnel." "Atlantis," unique, differs from the three other modern sections in founding itself on the healthiest aspects of the past and so rising to a vision of future possibilities.

Just as time is expanded in the poem, so too is space. The bridge moves from the East River first to span the ocean, then the continent, and finally to span the universe. This expanding bridge is in Crane's scheme always firmly assembled. And to emphasize his point makes all of his bridges elemental ones— structures that spring from earth, that bridge water, that are suspended in air, and that are fused into form through the agency of fire. Within the poem, consequently, space is compartmental- ized in very much the way time is compartmentalized; and though each section of the poem incorporates all four of the traditional elements of space, each section also stresses most strongly its own logically dominant element—water in "Ave Maria," for instance, or earth in "Powhatan's Daughter."

Finally, *The Bridge* is organized in terms of psychological and spiritual and aesthetic patterns. For just as man is compounded from the tensions of time and space—the oppositions of day and night, winter and summer, past and present; the opposition of water and shore, of earth and air, of fire and frost—so too he is compounded from Dionysian and Appollonian forces: freedom and restraint; a love that perpetually shuttles between passion and friendship; a God who sleeps in the earth and who awakens in vegetation ceremonies to ride the whirlwind and another God, apart, who searches cruelly with love his parable of man. For each of these oppositions, Crane also finds a voice. And since he is an artist, Crane fits into his poem, too, the oppositions which almost every artist is conscious of: the vision of art that is democratic, open, and objective and which Crane identifies with Whitman; and its counterpart and opposite, an art that is intensely personal, secret, subjective—the art of the symbolist tradition which Crane associates with Poe.

But though Crane assigns Whitman in "Cape Hatteras" to the Open Road and to the open air and links his name to summer and to comradeship and to joy—though Whitman becomes for him a symbol of life and though Poe, Whitman's opposite, is found trapped in the underground subjective subway on a very cold, drunken, dark December night, his eyes brim-full of death, we should not—indeed we must not—be led into the illusion that Crane finds one side of his design to be more praiseworthy than the other, or indeed that he fails to recognize that Whitman contains Poe and Poe, Whitman. Whitman and Poe, light and dark, joy and pain, life and death must—in Crane's scheme of things—finally both coexist and interpenetrate. For his bridge has two towers, each necessary for the support of the other. Only through the interaction of those opposed towers, as he points out at the end of "Atlantis," can the suspension—"One Song, one Bridge of Fire"—be achieved.

Unity seems finally to triumph; and as Crane brings his poem to an end, opposites harmoniously merge: "rainbows ring/ The serpent with the eagle in the leaves." But neither life nor death, neither land nor sea, neither present nor past can long remain fixed in such beautiful, hideous stasis, and in the last line of the poem Crane reminds us of that which we already know. Whispers hover through the cables of his bridge, warning us that already new appositions are forming in the midst of momentary order: From the two blazing towers of Crane's emerged white structure "Whispers *antiphonal* in azure *swing.*"

Glauco Cambon

From "Hart Crane's 'The Bridge'"

The proem ("To Brooklyn Bridge") stands somewhat apart, with its compressed quatrains hymning the main symbol, New York's well-known landmark—

> O harp and altar, of the fury fused,
> . . .
> Terrific threshold of the prophet's pledge,
> Prayer of pariah, and the lover's cry,——

which finally reveals itself as the divine archetype of poetical consciousness, soaring to span in its sleepless curve river, sea, and prairie, namely all of the world in space, all of time's order:

> O Sleepless as the river under thee,
> Vaulting the sea, the prairies' dreaming sod,
> Unto us lowliest sometimes sweep, descend
> And of the curveship lend a myth to God.

From *The Inclusive Flame: Studies in American Poetry* (Bloomington: Indiana University Press, 1963), pp. 132-44. Reprinted by permission of the publisher.

In the poem's epilogue ("Atlantis") the image of the bridge reappears consumed in a mystical fire that destroys its materiality,
transfiguring it into a harp of light, into ecstasy. From the viewpoint of structure (and of genesis, as we saw) truly *The Bridge*
can say of itself "In my beginning is my end." Some critics have
found difficulty with this symbolization of a mechanical object
which was ill equipped to bear such an investment of transcendental attributes; Crane, however, saw in that iron structure a
dynamic form instead of a static thing, for he felt, condensed in it,
the whole fury of a Faustian epoch. Besides, Brooklyn Bridge lived
in pictorial iconography; the painter, Joseph Stella, used it in a
famous Futurist-Cubist work which also brings out the formal
suggestion of a harp and of a Gothic cathedral, and he explained
in writing the reasons for his visual treatment, arousing Crane's
warm response in a letter now accessible in published form.
Mayakovsky's ode has already been mentioned, and that too goes
to show that if Brooklyn Bridge stimulated Crane's imagination,
it was no purely private event, despite his contrary misgivings.
The wealth of symbolic connotations he discovered, or poured out
on it, may at times be disconcerting, for it tends to clutter the
page with baroque redundancies; but this means that Crane's
problem was a crisis of richness rather than of poverty. And,
finally, a bridge *bridges;* the poet's imagination suffers no restric-
tion when it comes to feeling a suitable object as pure action.

The proem epitomizes the whole poem with subtle anticipa-
tions. It gives us the chaotic energy of the city, the breath of
oceans, the mystical afflatus, the linguistic violence that pervade
the whole work; and it rises to striking beauty, for instance, in
the first two quatrains, where the vision of seagulls circling the
Statue of Liberty in weird whiteness against the iron-gray background of the harbor dawn, with the Bridge itself as a perpetual
apparition to counterpoint it, evokes to the inner eye such a New
York as might have been painted by the demonic brush of Oscar
Kokoschka. The strength of these lines results from a tense balance between the stability of the bridge, full of arrested motion,
and the frenzy of the city culminating in the (autobiographically
prophetic) suicide of the madman:

> Out of some subway scuttle, cell or loft
> A bedlamite speeds to thy parapets,
> Tilting there momently, shrill shirt ballooning,
> A jest falls from the speechless caravan.

The violent atmosphere, swaying between outcry, dithyramb, and prayer, parallels very closely the most characteristic work of certain German expressionists, particularly Heym, Stadler, and Werfel.

As to the poetical validity of the bridge symbol, Sonia Raiziss makes the best case for it in *The Metaphysical Passion*,[1] where Crane is placed, along with other significant moderns, in the perspective of twentieth-century metaphysical poetry. Quoting from Henry Wells's *New Poets from Old*, she sees all of metaphysical art as a *bridge* spanning the finite and the infinite, the many and the one, past and future, the apparent chaos and the essential harmony of existence. This kind of poetry, according to her, rises as a mirror of, and response to, ages of climactic ideological conflict, like our century and the seventeenth. Paradoxical imagery seeks to hold together, without muffling them, the centrifugal pulls of an explosive reality; it is the crisis and the effort to overcome the crisis on the level of imagination. Thus the bridge does not appear in Crane's poem merely as its literal protagonist (despite the invocations he addresses to it), but because it concretely expresses the inner structure of the world Crane set out to explore. For the bridge, when we think of it as analogic form released from the weight of steel, is the metaphor, the linguistic and cognitive act of poetry as such—the only kind of unification Crane knew. This much remains true even if we feel that the bridge, in Crane's fiery addresses, is at times on the verge of becoming an idol. On one level, the poet extols in the language of worship a man-made thing, while endeavoring on the other to capture in it the human source of energy from which it arose, and the self-transcending drive of that energy. The simultaneities are enticingly precarious.

After this astonishing proem, which Waggoner and Wells agree in considering one of the most important lyrics in American literature, the poet's camera eye turns back four centuries and a half to enter the mind of Christopher Columbus on his first return trip to Spain from the newly discovered shore. The navigator is thinking of hardships met so far and of those he will still have to face at the hands of his royal patrons; of Ferdinand's greed, of the thirst for gold that may spoil the fruits of his conquest; he lifts his thought to the God Pneuma, manifested in the ocean wind, and to the Virgin Mary, protector of ships; he envisions the

[1]Sonia Raiziss, *The Metaphysical Passion* (Philadelphia, 1952), p. 19.

future crops of golden wheat and "pendant seething wheat of
knowledge" that may posthumously crown his fondest hopes, and
finally soars with prophetic imagination beyond any earthly reach,
into the fiery heart of God:

> Thy purpose—still one shore beyond desire!
> The sea's green crying towers a-sway, Beyond
>
> And kingdoms
>   naked in the
>   trembling heart—
> Te Deum laudamus
>   O Thou Hand of Fire.

This section, drawn from Columbus's diary through the splendid
mediation of William Carlos Williams' *In the American Grain*,
shows to great advantage Crane's mastery of language, his inspired sincerity, his musical and painterly sensibility. The sea—a
recurrent theme in his poetry, from *The Bridge* itself to "Voyages" and *Key West*—lives in these lines with dazzling force:

> Here waves climb into dusk on gleaming mail;
> Invisible valves of the sea,—locks, tendons
> Crested and creeping, troughing corridors
> That fall back yawning to another plunge.
> Slowly the sun's red caravel drops light
> Once more behind us. . . . It is morning there—

The marine rhythm, the brilliancy of that image of the sea as
the armor of a cataphract, which stresses the basic situation of
struggle against men and elements alike; the effectiveness of the
alliterations and internal echoes ("climb . . . gleaming;" "invisible
valves"; "crested . . . creeping . . . troughing . . . corridors"); the
movement of thought from imminent European dusk to the sunrise Columbus' ship left behind in the New World, which thereby
receives its proper connotations as the Land of the Morning, the
Orient he believed he had reached, and, at the same time, as the
new dawn of history to be found in the West, the world of the
new beginning; the subtle metaphor transforming the sun into a
heavenly caravel that analogically repeats Christopher's light-
bringing voyage to the new empires—everything contributes to
make these lines a tight, radiant tissue. We have already pointed
out the affinity of Crane's exuberant, exclamatory poetry to Ex-
pressionism; and it would be no contradiction to add that his
problem can best be defined by the critic as *grandeurs et misères*

du baroque, if we keep in mind Eugenio d'Ors's definition of baroque. For this is perhaps the truest stylistic portrait of Hart Crane as it emerges from failures and successes alike: a melter of forms, sensually and mystically effusive, forever spinning coils of thought and sound, vaulting sensory concreteness into abstraction and back again, from "Faustus and Helen" to "The Broken Tower." The incidental mannerism was well worth risking.

Many motifs in the Columbus section are interwoven with other parts of the rhapsody. They generate a kind of unity by interplay: for instance, the "white birds" of stanza 4 directly echo the seagulls of the proem and anticipate the eagles and airplanes of later sections. A closer look, however, shows deeper implications. The phrase "The Great White Birds!" is uttered by the natives of San Salvador at the approach of the majestic white-winged vessels, toward which they "came out . . . crying;" thus the passage fuses the seagull of the proem, stanza 1, with the "apparitional sails" of stanza 2. But the synthesis, chromatically based on the whiteness of birds and sails and spontaneously proposed by the animistic imagination of the primitive gazers, creates a new level of reality by raising Columbus' ships, crew and all, to the status of angels—which they certainly are as messengers of European civilization and, more specifically, of the Christian God. It is impossible to dismiss the suggestion that Crane here kept an eye on the sacramental etymology of the Genoese admiral's names: "Christ-bearer" (Christopher) and "Dove" (Colombus). However that may be, he did consciously enhance the angelic overtone of the sail imagery toward the rapturous end of the section, where he transfigured the ships into choirs of angels circling God:

> Elohim, still I hear thy sounding heel!
>
> White toil of heaven's cordons, mustering
> In holy rings all sails charged to the far
> Hushed gleaming fields. . . .

This imaginative climax anticipates the "white choiring wings" of "Atlantis," stanza 10, and reverberates on the beginning of the proem, where the seagull analogically circles the Statue of Liberty and conjures the fleeting memory of a remote, but still available, past: the "apparitional sails" of Columbian discovery, the great beginning, not to be lost.

The Virgin Mary with her "ageless blue" reappears in "Virginia" as blue-eyed Mary the typist, as Eternal Feminine in Pocahontas ("The Dance"), and in "Indiana" 's pioneer mother;

the Divine Hand of Fire re-emerges as erotic yearning in "The Harbor Dawn," then as a human guide at the end of "Cape Hatteras" ("My/ hand in yours, / Walt Whitman—/ so—"), and finally at the end of "The Tunnel":

> How far away the star has pooled the sea—
> Or shall the hands be drawn away, to die?
> Kiss of our agony Thou gatherest,
>   O Hand of Fire
>   gatherest—

Cathay, of course, runs through the whole poem to the climax of "Atlantis," where it blends with the informing idea of the bridge, with the mythical submerged continent and with the fire of God:

> One Song, one Bridge of Fire; Is it Cathay. . . .

Since Columbus thought he had reached China by inverting the customary route, this most provocative of historical mistakes allows Crane to identify the reality of geographic discovery with the driving force of vision, paradox with evidence, actual America with the America to be.

"Atlantis" becomes thus more understandable as the attempted consummation of the rhapsody—a consummation that seeks to achieve itself not merely on the sweeping plane of general idea, but through the intimate innervations of language. Comparison of "Atlantis" with "Ave Maria" will show how accurately the stanzas of the concluding section rehearse those of the opening one, merging the latter with the proem in one final thrust of prophecy. One capillary example: the "cordage tree" of "Ave Maria," stanza 7, line 5, in addition to being a fruitful vegetal pun in itself, visually supported by the essential shape of a ship-mast, develops into a different "cordage" in "Atlantis," stanza 2, line 1, where it summarizes the "bound cable strands," the "flight of strings," the "telepathy of wires," the "transparent meshes" that, in stanza 1, dynamically describe the design of the bridge as such. But since in the universe of expanding-interweaving metaphor the center is everywhere, this thematic relation is finally resolved in the ultimate theme of the poem; it is far more than clever word play, if we think that it projects the "cordage" or rigging of Columbus' ship into the lithe metal structures of Brooklyn Bridge, and thereby epiphanizes the idea that Columbus was himself a "bridge" between two worlds, while the present-day construction resumes, on another level, the same function as an actuality, yet also as a symbolic possibility.

To follow the ramifications of that "cordage tree" means, therefore, to trace the entire nervous system of Crane's ambitious poem. A pivotal echo rings in the last stanza of "Ave Maria":

> White *toil* of heaven's *cordons*, mustering
> In holy rings all sails. . . . [italics mine—G.C.]

Thus the metamorphic impulse transforms the tree-like image of the ship's mast and rigging into a net (compare the "transparent meshes" of the bridge in "Atlantis"). It is, however, a net of circles ("holy rings"), and this opens up a whole gamut of further possibilities, the more immediate one being directly exploited a few lines below:

> —The kindled Crown! acceded of the poles
> And biassed by full sails, *meridians reel* . . .[italics mine—G.C.]

The circular network of meridians and parallels mathematically defines the globe around which Columbus was sailing, and at the same time manifests in its inclusive form the completeness of God, the Bridge of Bridges, spanning all distances, as the last line of stanza 9 had proclaimed:

> Te Deum laudamus, for thy teeming span!

Besides, meridians and parallels are mere abstractions of map geometry; they become perceptible by analogy, for a navigator, as the shifting horizon line that determines his position on the sea and that he, in his turn, determines by his course; thus the mystical-geometric metaphors of "Ave Maria's" last stanza bring us back to the vividly pictorial experience of stanza 6:

> Series on series, infinite,—till eyes
> Starved wide on blackened tides, accrete—enclose
> This *turning rondure whole*, this *crescent ring*
> Sun-cusped and zoned with modulated fire
> Like pearls that whisper through the Doge's hands
> —Yet no delirium of jewels! [italics mine—G.C.]

We note the symbolic inherences: man's eyes (a recurrent leit-motif of the rhapsody) enclose and are enclosed by the like shape of macrocosm in the act of exploration, or knowledge, that aquires in itself a round shape; and roundness connects, in the chain of being, pearls, eyes, horizon, earth, planets, sun, and the heavenly vault. This manifests the full potential of the bridge, which, at the end of the proem, had been implored to "of [thy] curveship lend a myth to God"; the curvature of four-dimensional space, for Crane, who absorbed Einstein's ideas through the visionary mediation of Ouspensky, embodying as such the godlike experience of totality.

But we are not yet done with the interlocking analogies that sprout up in every direction from the initially chosen point: those "pearls" and "jewels" start another chain reaction in stanza 9, with "Teneriffe's garnet," and in stanza 10, where we find

> This disposition that thy night relates
> From Moon to Saturn in one sapphire wheel. . . .

"Teneriffe's garnet," a vivid metaphor for the volcano Columbus met on his way to America, takes up the imagistic cues of "jewels" and "modulated fire" from the previously quoted passage of stanza 6 to merge them into one, and transcends both again by resolving the achieved crystallization into the concrete sight of a volcanic eruption:

> And Teneriffe's garnet—flamed it in a cloud,
> Urging through night our passage to the Chan; . . . .

The metaphoric impulse never stands still, and relates the volcano to the pillar of fire that guided the Hebrews by night and the cloud that guided them by day, while the tactical appearance of the Chan, Cathay's emperor, picks up in its own right the jewelry cue; two stanzas below, fire, smoke cloud, kingly attributes, stars, and jewelry will blend into one flash of telescoped images that gives us God in the act of full revelation or, so to speak, "unclouding":

> . . .—round thy brows unhooded now
> —The kindled Crown!

The real King supersedes his earthly counterparts: Ferdinand of Spain, avid for earthly jewels, and the Khan of Cathay, reigning over fabled riches; the Crown (astronomically, Corona Borealis) has become the "rondure whole" of the ultimate "Curveship," and echoes directly the "sapphire wheel" of stanza 10, with its immediate development:

> The orbic wake of thy once whirling feet. . . .

It may also be worth noticing that the sapphire's canonic attribute with regard to splendor and purity is "oriental," so that in this context it would seem to connote the shining kingdom of Cathay, while on the other hand, as Crane may have seen in Webster's dictionary, the word "sapphire" itself is etymologically related to Saturn. "From Moon to Saturn": heavenly bodies are important to a navigator even if he has, like Columbus, a compass to rely on; but then, the "true appointment" yielded by the magnetic needle of line 2 in this stanza becomes a multivalent "disposition" in line 5, thereby acquiring an astrological connotation that suggests the bridging of lunar femininity and saturnine masculinity, as well as the conjunction of good and bad luck (the moon's phases being used in astrology to determine by calculation propitious and unfavorable days, while Saturn was considered "infortune" or malevolent). Astronomically speaking, Saturn has a ring that would not be ignored in this context, and apart from that, it derives its name from the Roman god of time, of the golden age, of harvest, thus relating to the "pendant seething wheat" and "hushed fields" of the following stanza, and by the same token to the "ripe fields" and "harvests" of "Atlantis," stanza 9. Taking into account the function of the moon as ageless time-measurer and Saturn as time god, we may find the "amplitude that time explores" of line 1 locally echoed in the line that conjoins the two planets, with a possible overtone of the week pattern ("from Monday to Saturday") to introduce the idea of a cycle to be crowned by "Sunday," the day of the Sun and of the Lord, who appears as Elohim two lines below. Whichever way we look, we get the idea of completion, of what Dickinson would have called "circumference," and a spatial aspect can be added to it by recalling that, in ancient cosmology, the moon was the closest and Saturn the farthest of the planets: thus the "sapphire wheel" encircles the solar system itself.

The endlessly intertwining ramifications of the "cordage tree" have branched out into the cosmos, but always with a bearing on the central idea of "bridges." One particularly felicitous development takes place, as has been pointed out before, in the proem as well as in "Atlantis," where that "cordage" vibrantly shades into the strings of a harp. In those privileged moments, without losing sight of the visual object before him (the bridge), Hart Crane can project man's music (his own as well as the shriller one of his culture as a whole) into the music of the spheres, because the harp at that point epitomizes the entire cosmos. Columbus, the man of science and faith, provides the particular focus in "Ave Maria," yet as navigator he reappears in the sailor of "Cutty Sark" as explorer in the tramps of "The River," and in the Larry of "Indiana," as embodied yearning for knowledge in Walt Whitman ("Cape Hatteras"), and in Crane himself. Columbus had been a natural archetype in American poetry long before Williams and Crane dramatized him; Joel Barlow's *The Vision of Columbus* is an especially poignant antecedent because it shows the Genoese seafarer contemplating, from a hilltop where he has come to rest and die, the great future of America, but Philip Freneau's Pictures of Columbus" should also be remembered, along with Washington Irving's copious volumes on Columbus and on his companions. Finally, Whitman's "Prayer of Columbus" has to be taken into account, given Crane's affinity for Walt, in a perspective focused on *The Bridge*. Undoubtedly Crane responded felicitously to this theme because he felt it from the inside, aided by a sustaining American tradition. Columbus spontaneously became in his hands a focal symbol of the human mind venturing into new horizons—something comparable to the Ulysses archetype in Ezra Pound's *Cantos*, whose very beginning is deftly varied in the cadence of "Ave Maria" 's fourth stanza. . . .

Alan Trachtenberg

The Shadow of a Myth

> *Oh, grassy glades! oh, ever vernal endless*
> *landscapes in the soul; in ye,—men yet may roll,*
> *like young horses in new morning clover; and for some*
> *few fleeting moments, feel the cool dew*
> *of the life immortal on them. Would to God*
> *these blessed calms would last.*

> HERMAN MELVILLE, *Moby-Dick* (1851)

> *The time is barren, and therefore its poet overrich.*

> MARTIN HEIDEGGER, "Hölderlin and the Nature of Poetry" (1937)

In the winter of 1923, Hart Crane, a twenty-four-year-old poet living in Cleveland, announced plans to write a long poem called *The Bridge*. It was to be an epic, a "mystical synthesis of Amer-

---

From *Brooklyn Bridge: Fact and Symbol* (New York: Oxford University Press, 1965), pp. 142-65. Copyright © 1965 by Alan Trachtenberg. Reprinted by permission of Oxford University Press, Inc.

113

ica."[1] Crane had just completed *For the Marriage of Faustus and Helen*, a poem which sought to infuse modern Faustian culture (the term was Spengler's, designating science and restless searching) with love of beauty and religious devotion. Now, confirmed in his commitment to visionary poetry and feeling "directly connected with Whitman," Crane prepared for an even greater effort: to compose the myth of America. The poem would answer "the complete renunciation symbolized in *The Waste Land*," published the year before. Eliot had used London Bridge as a passageway for the dead, on which "each man fixed his eyes before his feet." Crane replied by projecting his myth of affirmation upon Brooklyn Bridge.

In the spring of 1923, Hart Crane left his father's home in Cleveland, and from then until his suicide in 1932, lived frequently in Brooklyn Heights, close to "the most beautiful Bridge of the world." He crossed the bridge often, alone and with friends, sometimes with lovers: "the cables enclosing us and pulling us upward in such a dance as I have never walked and never can walk with another." Part III of *Faustus and Helen* had been set in the shadow of the bridge, "where," Crane wrote, "the edge of the bridge leaps over the edge of the street." In the poem the bridge is the "Capped arbiter of beauty in this street," "the ominous lifted arm / That lowers down the arc of Helen's brow." Its "curve" of "memory" transcends "all stubble streets."

Crane tried to keep Brooklyn Bridge always before him, in eye as well as in mind. In April 1924 he wrote: "I am now living in the shadow of the bridge." He had moved to 110 Columbia Heights, into the very house, and later, the very room occupied fifty years earlier by Roebling. Like the crippled engineer, the

[1] *The Bridge* was first published by The Black Sun Press, Paris, 1930; this edition included three photographs by Walker Evans. The lines quoted throughout this chapter are from *The Complete Poems of Hart Crane* (New York, 1933), ed., Waldo Frank; references in the chapter are to *The Letters of Hart Crane* (New York, 1952), ed., Brom Weber. The critical works I have profited from most in my reading of *The Bridge* are, Allen Tate, "Hart Crane," *Reactionary Essays* (New York, 1936); Yvor Winters, "The Significance of *The Bridge*," *In Defense of Reason* (New York, 1947), 575–605; R. P. Blackmur, "New Thresholds, New Anatomies: Notes on a Text of Hart Crane," *Language as Gesture* (New York, 1952); Brom Weber, *Hart Crane: A Biographical and Critical Study* (New York, 1948); L. S. Dembo, *Hart Crane's Sanskrit Charge: A Study of The Bridge* (Ithaca, 1960); Sister M. Bernetta Quinn, *The Metamorphic Tradition in Modern Poetry* (New Brunswick, 1955), 130–68; Stanley K. Coffman, "Symbolism in *The Bridge*," *PMLA*, Vol. LXVI (March 1951), 65–77; John Unterecker, "The Architecture of The Bridge," *Wisconsin Studies in Contemporary Literature*. Vol. III (Spring–Summer 1962), 5–20.

poet was to devote his most creative years to the vision across the harbor. In his imagination the shadow of the bridge deepened into the shadow of a myth.

I

The Bridge, Crane wrote, carries further the tendencies manifest in 'F and H.' " These tendencies included a neo-Platonic conception of a "reality" beyond the evidence of the senses. The blind chaos of sensation in the modern city apparently denies this transcendent reality, but a glimpse of it is available, through ecstasy, to the properly devout poet. Helen represents the eternal, the unchanging; Faustus, the poet's aspiration; and the "religious gunman" of Part III, spirit of the Dionysian surrender (sexual as well as aesthetic) necessary for a vision of the eternal. The threefold image constitutes what Kenneth Burke has called an "aesthetic myth"—a modern substitute for "religious myth."[2] The poet's impulse toward beauty is a mark of divinity. A part of the myth, and another "tendency" of the poem, is what Crane called its "fusion of our time with the past." The past is represented by the names Faustus and Helen; the present by the data of the poem: the "memoranda," the "baseball scores," and "stock quotations" of Part I; the jazz dance of Part II; the warplanes of Part III. The present fails to live up to the past. But the poet, a "bent axle of devotion," keeps his "lone eye" riveted upon Helen; he offers her "one inconspicuous, glowing orb of praise." At the end, in communion with the "religious gunman," he accepts and affirms past and present, the "years" whose "hands" are bloody; he has attained "the height/ The imagination spans beyond despair."

The idea of a bridge is explicit in the closing image; earlier, as I have indicated, it had appeared in fact, leaping over the street. In the projected poem, it will leap far beyond the street, but its function will be similar: an emblem of the eternal, providing a passage between the Ideal and the transitory sensations of history, a way to unify them.

In the earliest lines written for the new poem, the bridge was the location of an experience like that which ends *Faustus and Helen*: the imagination spanning beyond despair.

> And midway on that structure I would stand
> One moment, not as diver, but with arms

---

[2] *A Rhetoric of Motives* (New York, 1950), 203.

That open to project a disk's resilience
Winding the sun and planets in its face.

           *   *   *

Expansive center, pure moment and electron
That guards like eyes that must look always down
In reconcilement of our chains and ecstasy
Crashing manifoldly on us as we hear
The looms, the wheels, the whistles in concord
Tethered and welded as the hills of dawn . . .[3]

Somewhat like Wordsworth on Westminister Bridge, here the poet experiences harmony, his troubled self annihilated in a moment of worship. Subsequently Crane developed a narrative to precede this experience. In the narrative, or myth, the poet, like Faustus, was to be the hero, and his task a quest—not for Helen but her modern equivalent: Brooklyn Bridge.

Although the bridge lay at the end of quest, it was not, like the grail in *The Waste Land*, simply a magical object occupying a given location. It does not wait to be found, but to be created. That is, it represents not an external "thing," but an internal process, an act of consciousness. The bridge is not "found" in "Atlantis," the final section of the poem, but "made" throughout the poem. In "Atlantis" what has been "made" is at last recognized and named: "O Thou steeled Cognizance." Its properties are not magical but conceptual: it is a "Paradigm" of love and beauty, the eternal ideas which lie behind and inform human experience.

If we follow the poet's Platonic idea, to "think" the bridge is to perceive the unity and wholeness of history. In the poem, history is not chronological nor economic nor political. Crane wrote: "History and fact, location, etc., all have to be transfigured into abstract form that would almost function independently of its subject matter." Crane intended to re-create American history according to a pattern he derived from its facts. His version of American history has nothing in common with the ceremonial parade of Founding Fathers and bearded generals of popular culture. The poet's idea, and especially his distinction between history and "abstract form," is closer to what the anthropologist Mircea Eliade describes as the predominant ontology of archaic

---

[3] The first four lines are from "Lines sent to Wilbur Underwood, February, 1923," and the remainder from "Worksheets, Spring, 1923," in Brom Weber, *Hart Crane.* 425–6.

man—the myth of "eternal return." According to Eliade, the mind of archaic man sought to resist history—the line of "irreversible events"—by re-creating, in his rituals, the pre-temporal events of his mythology, such as the creation of the world. Unable to abide a feeling of uniqueness, early men identified, in their rituals, the present with the mythic past, thus abolishing the present as an autonomous moment of time. All events and actions "acquire a value," writes Eliade, "and in so doing become real, because they participate, after one fashion or another, in a reality that transcends them." The only "real" events are those recorded in mythology, which in turn become models for imitation, "paradigmatic gestures." All precious stones are precious because of thunder from heaven; all sacred buildings are sacred because they are built over the divine Center of the world; all sexual acts repeat the primordial act of creation. A non-precious stone, a non-sacred building, a non-sanctified act of sex—these are not real. History, as distinct from myth, consists of such random acts and events, underived from an archetype; therefore history is not real and must be periodically "annulled." By imitating the "paradigmatic gesture" in ritual, archaic men transported themselves out of the realm of the random, of "irreversible events," and "re-actualized" the mythic epoch in which the original archetypal act occurred. Hence for the primitive as for the mystic, time has no lasting influence: "events repeat themselves because they imitate an archetype." Like the mystic, the primitive lives in a "continual present."[4]

The Bridge is a sophisticated and well-wrought version of the archaic myth of return. The subject matter of the poem is drawn from legends about American history: Columbus, Pocahontas, Cortez, De Soto, Rip Van Winkle, the gold-rush, the whalers; and from contemporary reality: railroads, subways, warplanes, office buildings, cinemas, burlesque queens. Woven among these strands are allusions to world literature: the Bible, Plato, Marlowe, Shakespeare, Blake; and most important, to American artists: Whitman, Melville, Poe, Dickinson, Isadora Duncan. The action of the poem comprises through its fifteen sections, one waking day, from dawn in "Harbor Dawn," to midnight in "Atlantis." Through the device of dream, that single day includes vast stretches of time and space: a subway ride in the morning extends to a railroad journey to the Mississippi, then back in time, beyond De Soto, to the

4 *Cosmos and History: The Myth of the Eternal Return* (Harper Torchbooks, 1959), 4, 90.

primeval world of the Indians,[5] then forward to the West of the pioneers. In a sense, the entire day is a dream; the poet journeys through his own consciousness toward an awakening. He seeks to learn the meaning of American history which, in so far as that history is inseparable from his own memories, is the meaning of himself: Cathay, which designates the end of the journey, or the discovery of a new world, Crane wrote, is "an attitude of spirit," a self-discovery.

Thus in no sense of the word is *The Bridge* a historical poem. Its mode is myth. Its aim is to overcome history, to abolish time and the autonomy of events, and to show that all meaningful events partake of an archetype: the quest for a new world. In this regard the importance of Walt Whitman requires special notice. For among the many influences that worked upon Crane, few were as persuasive as Whitman's.[6]

---

[5] Crane's conception of the Indian in "The Dance"—in the "Powhatan's Daughter" section of *The Bridge*—seems to owe something to Waldo Frank's *Our America* (1919). In his personal copy, Crane had underlined the following passage: "His [the Indian's] magic is not, as in most religions, the tricky power of men over their gods. It lies in the power of Nature herself to yield corn from irrigation, to yield meat in game. The Indian therefore does not pray to his God for direct favors. He prays for harmony between himself and the mysterious forces that surround him: of which he is one. For he has learned that from this harmony comes health." Hart Crane Collection, Columbia University Library.

[6] A word should be said about the powerful influence upon Crane's sensibility—and his plans for *The Bridge*—of the Russian mystic, P. D. Ouspensky, and his work, *Tertium Organum: The Third Canon of Thought. A Key to the Enigmas of the World.* tr. Nicholas Bessaraboff and Claude Bragdon (New York, 1922). Crane read this book early in his creative life—possibly in 1920 (an earlier edition had been published that year). It seems very likely that he derived most of his philosophical idealism, and a good deal of his language and imagery, from Ouspensky. A case could be made for the fact that he interpreted Whitman in Ouspenskian terms—as a mystic who saw through the world to a higher reality. "Higher consciousness" was a typical Ouspenskian term. So was "vision," in its literal and metaphoric senses. Plato's parable of the cave, in which most men sit in darkness, hidden from the truth, is the unstated assumption of Ouspensky's book. The book attempts to place the mystical experience of light and oneness on accountable grounds; its method is to prove by analogies that the true or noumenal world lies beyond space and time, beyond the capacity of the normal mind to perceive. Limited to a three-dimensional view of the world (a consequence of education and bad science), the mind normally interprets what are really flashes from the true world as things moving in time. In truth, however, the "whole" is motionless and self-contained; time itself is man's illusion: "The idea of time recedes with the expansion of consciousness." The true world being "invisible" to normal sight, it is necessary to cultivate the inner eye. This can be accomplished only by exercising the outer eye to its fullest capacities—to strain vision until familar things seem unfamiliar, new, and exciting. Then we might penetrate the "hidden meaning in everything." Then we will see the "invisible threads" which bind all

In "Passage to India," we have seen, Whitman identified the quest for wholeness—the "rondure"—as the chief theme and motive of American life. In Whitman's version of history, man was expelled from Eden into time: "Wandering, yearning, curious, with restless explorations,/ With questions, baffled, formless, feverish." Divided into separate and warring nations, at odds with nature, historical man was a sufferer. Now, however, in modern America, the end of suffering was in sight. The connecting works of engineers—the Suez Canal, the Atlantic Cable, the Union Pacific Railroad—had introduced a new stage; the separate geographical parts of the world were now linked into one system. The physical labors of engineers, moreover, were spiritual food for the poet; the "true son of God" recognized that by uniting East and West such works completed Columbus's voyage. Now it was clear: The "hidden" purpose of history was the brotherhood of races that would follow the bridges and canals of modern technology.

Crane was not interested principally in Whitman's social vision, but in his conception of poetry as the final step in the restoration of man's wholeness. Not the engineer nor the statesman nor the captain of industry, but the poet was the true civilizer. Translating engineering accomplishments into ideas, the poet completed the work of history, and prepared for the ultimate journey to "more than India," the journey to the Soul: "thou actual Me." Thus the poet recognized that all of history culminated in self-discovery; and he would lead the race out of its bondage in time and space to that moment of consciousness in which all would seem one. That moment of "return" would redeem history by abolishing it. In short, Crane inherited from Whitman the belief in the poet's function to judge history from the point of view of myth.

Whitman himself appears in "Cape Hatteras," which represents a critical phase of the action of *The Bridge.* In the preceding sections, the poet had set out to find Pocahontas, the spirit of the land. With Rip Van Winkle his Muse of Memory, and the

---

things together—"with the entire world, with all the past and all the future." It should be noted that an idea of a bridge is implicit here—a metaphoric bridge which represents the true unity of all things. Moreover, Ouspensky held that art, especially poetry, was a means to attain this metaphoric bridge. To do so, however, poetry must develop a new language: "New parts of speech are necessary, an infinite number of new words." The function of poetry is to reveal the "invisible threads," to translate them into language which will "bind" the reader to the new perceptions. It is quite easy to see how attractive these ideas were to Hart Crane's poetic program. See Weber, 150–63.

Twentieth Century Limited his vehicle, he moved westward out
of the city to the Mississippi, the river of time. Borne backward
on the stream, he found the goddess, joined her dance of union
with nature, and thus entered the archetype. Now he must return
to the present, to bridge the personal vision of the goddess and
the actuality of modern America. An older sailor (possibly Melville) in a South Street bar and an apparition of old clipper ships
from Brooklyn Bridge in "Cutty Sark," are reminders of the quest.
But the old has lost its direction; the age requires a renewal.

"Cape Hatteras" is the center of the span that leaps from
Columbus to Brooklyn Bridge. The sea voyages are now done, the
rondure accomplished. Now, a complacent age of stocks, traffic,
and radios has lost sight of its goal; instead of a bridge, the age has
created "a labyrinth submersed/ Where each sees only his dim
past reversed." War, not peace and brotherhood, has succeeded
the engineers, and flights into space are undertaken, not by poets
but by war planes. "Cape Hatteras" poses the key questions of the
poem: "What are the grounds for hope that modern history will
not destroy itself?" "Where lies redemption?" "Is there an alternative to the chaos of the City?"

The answers are in Whitman's "sea eyes," "bright with myth."
He alone has kept sight of the abstract form, the vision of ultimate
integration. His perspective is geological; he stands apart, with
"something green,/ Beyond all sesames of science." Whitman
envisioned the highest human possibilities within the facts of
chaos. It was he who "stood up and flung the span on even wing/
Of that great Bridge, our Myth, whereof I sing." He is a presence:
"Familiar, thou, as mendicants in public places." He has kept
faith, even among the most disastrous circumstances of betrayal.
With his help, the flight into space might yet become "that span
of consciousness thou'st named/ The Open Road."

"Cape Hatteras" introduces the violence and the promise, the
despair and the hope, of modern life. It argues for the effectiveness
of ideals, for the power of Utopia over history. The poet places his
hand in Whitman's, and proceeds upon his quest. Returning from
the sea in "Southern Cross," he searches for love in "National
Winter Garden" and "Virginia," for community and friendship in
"Quaker Hill," and for art in "The Tunnel." He finds nothing but
betrayal: the strip tease dancer burlesques Pocahontas, the office
girl is a pallid Mary, the New Avalon Hotel and golf course mock
the New England tradition, and the tunnel crucifies Poe. But
throughout, the poet's hand is in Whitman's, and at last, having
survived the terrors of "The Tunnel," he arrives at the bridge.

II

Brooklyn Bridge lay at the end of the poet's journey, the pledge of a "cognizance" that would explain and redeem history. To reach the bridge, to attain its understanding, the poet suffered the travail of hell. But he emerges unscathed, and ascends the span. In "Atlantis" he reaches Cathay, the symbol of sublime consciousness. The entire action implies a steady optimism that no matter how bad history may be, the bridge will reward the struggle richly. Such is its promise in the opening section of the poem, "Proem: To Brooklyn Bridge."

> How many dawns, chill from his rippling rest
> The seagull's wings shall dip and pivot him,
> Shedding white rings of tumult, building high
> Over the chained bay waters Liberty—
>
> Then, with inviolate curve, forsake our eyes
> As apparitional as sails that cross
> Some page of figures to be filed away;
> —Till elevators drop us from our day . . .
>
> I think of cinemas, panoramic sleights
> With multitudes bent toward some flashing scene
> Never disclosed, but hastened to again,
> Foretold to other eyes on the same screen;
>
> And Thee, across the harbor, silver-paced
> As though the sun took step of thee, yet left
> Some motion ever unspent in thy stride,—
> Implicitly thy freedom staying thee!
>
> Out of some subway scuttle, cell or loft
> A bedlamite speeds to thy parapets,
> Titling there momently, shrill shirt ballooning,
> A jest falls from the speechless caravan.
>
> Down Wall, from girder into street noon leaks,
> A rip-tooth of the sky's acetylene;
> All afternoon the cloud-flown derricks turn . . .
> Thy cables breathe the North Atlantic still.
>
> And obscure as that heaven of the Jews,
> Thy guerdon . . . Accolade thou dost bestow
> Of anonymity time cannot raise:
> Vibrant reprieve and pardon thou dost show.
>
> O harp and altar, of the fury fused,
> (How could mere toil align thy choiring strings!)
> Terrific threshold of the prophet's pledge,
> Prayer of pariah, and the lover's cry,—

Again the traffic lights that skim thy swift
Unfractioned idiom, immaculate sigh of stars,
Beading thy path—condense eternity:
And we have seen night lifted in thine arms.

Under thy shadow by the piers I waited;
Only in darkness is thy shadow clear.
The City's fiery parcels all undone,
Already snow submerges an iron year . . .

O Sleepless as the river under thee,
Vaulting the sea, the prairies' dreaming sod,
Unto us lowliest sometime sweep, descend
And of the curveship lend a myth to God.

The setting of "Proem" in the harbor and lower Manhattan area is distinct, though the point of view shifts a good deal within this area, from a long view of the Bay and the Statue of Liberty, to an office in a skyscraper, down an elevator into the street, into a dark movie house, and then to the sun-bathed bridge. The view of the bridge also changes, from "across the harbor," in which the sun appears to be walking up the diagonal stays, to the promenade and towers as the bedlamite "speeds to thy parapets." Later the point of view is under the bridge, in its shadow. The shifting perspectives secure the object in space; there is no question that it is a bridge across a river between two concretely realized cities.

At the same time, the bridge stands apart from its setting, a world of its own. A series of transformations in the opening stanzas bring us to it. We begin with a seagull at dawn—a specific occurrence, yet eternal ("How many dawns"). The bird's wings leave our eyes as an "inviolate curve" (meaning unprofaned as well as unbroken) to become "apparitional as sails" (apparitional implies "epiphanal" as well as spectral and subjective). Then, in a further transmutation, they become a "page of figures." As the wings leave our eyes, so does the page: "filed away." Then, elevators "drop us" from the bird to the street. In the shift from bird to page to elevator, we have witnessed the transformation of a curve into a perpendicular, of an organism into a mechanism— wings into a list of numbers. "Filed away," the vision of the curve, identified with "sails" and voyages, has been forgotten ("How many" times?), like a page of reckonings. The quest for a vision of bird and sails resumes in the cinema, but, as in Plato's cave, the "flashing scene" is "never disclosed." Then, the eye finds a permanent vision of the curve in the "silver-paced" bridge.

The bridge has emerged from a counterpoint of motions (bird vs. elevator; sails vs. "multitudes bent") as an image of self-containment. Surrounded by a frantic energy ("some flashing scene . . . hastened to again"; "A bedlamite speeds . . .") the bridge is aloof; its motions express the sun. Verbs like drop, tilt, leak, submerge describe the city; the bridge is rendered by verbs like turn, breathe, lift, sweep. Established in its own visual plane, with a motion of its own, the bridge is prepared, by stanza seven, to receive the epithets of divinity addressed to it. Like Mary, it embraces, reprieves, and pardons. Its cables and towers are "harp and altar." The lights of traffic along its roadway, its "unfractioned idiom," seem to "condense eternity." Finally, as night has extinguished the cities and thereby clarified the shadow of the bridge, its true meaning becomes clear: its "curveship" represents an epiphany, a myth to manifest the divine. Such at least is what the poet implores the bridge to be.

In "Proem," Brooklyn Bridge achieves its status in direct opposition to the way of life embodied in the cities. Bridge and city are opposing and apparently irreconcilable forms of energy. This opposition, which is equivalent to that between myth and history, continues through the remainder of the poem; it creates the local tensions of each section, and the major tension of the entire work.

This tension is best illustrated in "The Tunnel," the penultimate section of the poem. After a fruitless search for reality in a Times Square theater, the protagonist boards a subway as "the quickest promise home." The short ride to Brooklyn Bridge is a nightmare of banal conversations and advertisements: "To brush some new presentiment of pain." The images are bizarre: "and love/ A burnt match skating in a urinal." Poe appears, his head "swinging from the swollen strap," his eyes "Below the toothpaste and the dandruff ads." The crucified poet, dragged to his death through the streets of Baltimore, "That last night on the ballot rounds," represents how society uses its visionary devotees of beauty.[7]

---

[7] It is wrong to assume that Poe and Whitman oppose each other in this work—one gloomy, the other cheerful. Poe in the tunnel does indeed represent the actuality of art in modern life, but the image is not meant to contradict Whitman's vision—perhaps to countervail it, and by so doing, to reinforce its strength. According to his friends—especially Samuel Loveman—Crane loved both poets, although he derived more substance for his art from Whitman (and Melville). To make this point may also be a good occasion to recall that Whitman himself was powerfully drawn to Poe.

If the "Proem" promised deliverance, "The Tunnel" seems to deliver damnation; its chief character is a Daemon, whose "hideous laughter" is "the muffled slaughter of a day in birth." The Daemon's joke is that he has inverted the highest hopes and brightest prophecies: "O cruelly to inoculate the brinking dawn/ With antennae toward worlds that glow and sink." The presiding spirit in the tunnel, he represents the transvaluation of ideals in modern America.

At the end of "The Tunnel," the protagonist leaves the subway and prepares, at the water's edge, to ascend the bridge. His faith, like Job's, is unimpaired. Job endured the assault of Satan, uttered no complaints, and in the end profited by an enlightened understanding, albeit an irrational one, of the power of his God. It is revealing—although it has been largely unnoticed—that Crane's epigraph to *The Bridge* is taken from Satan's reply to God in Job, 1.7: "From going to and fro in the earth, and from walking up and down in it." The words might be read to indicate the theme of voyage, but their source suggests a richer interpretation: the omnipresence of evil, of the Daemon of "The Tunnel." Job's only defense is unremitting faith in his own righteousness and God's justice. And the same holds for the poet: faith in Whitman, his own powers, and in his bridge.

III

To keep the faith but not close his eyes to reality was Hart Crane's chief struggle in composing *The Bridge*. Reality in the 1920's—the age of jazz, inflated money, and Prohibition—did not

---

There is some evidence they knew each other as newspaper men in New York in the 1840's. Whitman was the only major American writer to attend the dedication of a Poe memorial in Baltimore in 1875, and sat on the platform as Mallarmé's famous poem was being read. In *Specimen Days,* Whitman wrote that Poe's verse expressed the "sub-currents" of the age; his poems were "lurid dreams." Thus, Poe presented an "entire contrast and contradiction" to the image of "perfect and noble life" which Whitman himself had tried to realize. But it is significant that Whitman concedes morbidity to be as true of the times as health. He tells of a dream he once had of a "superb little schooner" yacht, with "torn sails and broken spars," tossed in a stormy sea at midnight. "On the deck was a slender, slight, beautiful figure, a dim man, apparently enjoying all the terror, the murk, and the dislocation of which he was the center and the victim. That figure of my lurid dream might stand for Edgar Poe" (*Complete Prose Works,* 150). Whitman's "lurid dream" may very well be a source for Crane's nightmare in "The Tunnel"—where once more Poe is "the center and the victim." Much of the power of both images comes from the fact that, as Jack McManis has said to me, "Whitman's head [or Crane's] also could be swinging from that subway strap."

seem to support any faith let alone one like Crane's. It was a period of frantic construction, of competition for the title of "Tallest Building in the World," won in 1930 by the Empire State Building. That tower had climbed the sky at the rate of a story a day to the height of a hundred and two floors. Elsewhere, Florida experienced a hysterical real-estate boom. In 1927 the first cross-country highway announced the age of the automobile. The same year, Lindbergh crossed the Atlantic. And in the same decade, the movie palace spread into neighborhoods.

In certain moods, Crane was possessed by the fever of the period: "Time and space is the myth of the modern world," he wrote about Lindbergh, "and it is interesting to see how any victory in the field is heralded by the mass of humanity. In a way my Bridge is a manifestation of the same general subject. Maybe I'm just a little jealous of Lindy!"[8] But the over-all effect of the direction of American life did not accord with his myth. From 1926 to 1929, years during which his own physical and emotional life deteriorated noticeably,[9] Crane searched for a way to acknowledge the unhappy reality of America without surrendering his faith. The changes he made in the final poem of the sequence—the poem he had begun in 1923 and altered time and again—disclose the accommodation he reached.

At first, as I have indicated, the finale projected an intense experience of harmony. As his conception of the bridge took shape, he changed the ending accordingly, weaving into it the major images developed earlier, which are mainly nautical and musical. He reorganized the section into a walk across the bridge, and incorporated many structural details of the cables and towers. "I have attempted to induce the same feelings of elation, etc.—like being carried forward and upward simultaneously—both in imagery, rhythm and repetition, that one experiences in walking across my beloved Brooklyn Bridge."

> Through the bound cable strands, the arching path
> Upward, veering with light, the flight of strings,—
> Taut miles of shuttling moonlight syncopate
> The whispered rush, telepathy of wires.
> Up the index of night, granite and steel—
> Transparent meshes—fleckless the gleaming staves—

[8] Hart Crane to his father, June 21, 1927. Yale American Literature Collection.
[9] See Philip Horton, *Hart Crane: The Life of an American Poet* (New York, 1937).

Sibylline voices flicker, waveringly stream
As though a god were issue of the strings. . . .

                        *   *   *

Sheerly the eyes, like seagulls stung with rime—
Slit and propelled by glistening fins of light—
Pick biting way up towering looms that press
Sidelong with flight of blade on tendon blade
—Tomorrows into yesteryear—and link
What cipher-script of time no traveller reads

Rhythm and imagery convey a real bridge as well as an "arc synoptic": the walk across the span recapitulates the experience of the concluding day.

In stanza six, at the center of the roadway, the poet attains his vision. It is midnight; night is lifted "to cycloramic crest/ Of deepest day." Now, as "Tall Vision-of-the-Voyage," the bridge becomes a "Choir, translating time/ Into what multitudinous Verb": it is "Psalm of Cathay!/ O Love, thy white pervasive Paradigm. . . !" This moment is the climax of the poem. In the six stanzas which follow, Crane interprets the "multitudinous Verb" as the explicit action of reaching Cathay. He achieves this through predominant images of voyage; the bridge becomes a ship which, in stanza seven, "left the haven hanging in the night." The past tense modulates the tone of the entire section, for we are now "Pacific here at time's end, bearing corn." We have left the physical bridge, and are transported to another realm, a realm which fuses land ("corn") and water ("Pacific")—or Pocahontas and Columbus. The implied image is clearly that of an island, much like the "insular Tahiti" of the soul which Ishmael discovers to his salvation in Melville's *Moby-Dick*. The *Pequod* too had rushed ahead "from all havens astern." In stanza eleven, the poet like the lone survivor of Ahab's madness, finds himself "floating" on the waters, his visionary Belle Isle (Atlantis) sustaining him. In the last stanza, still addressing the bridge, he floats onward toward Cathay. The passage has been made "from time's realm" to "time's end" to "thine Everpresence, beyond time." Like Melville, Crane began his spiritual voyage in the North Atlantic, plunged into older waters, and nearing Cathay, recovered the even older shores of Atlantis. East and West have merged in a single chrysalis.

The language of the closing six stanzas of the section has the resonance of a hymn; it includes some of Crane's most quoted epithets: "Unspeakable Thou Bridge to Thee, O Love." But the oracular tone is bought at an expense. The opening six stanzas were dominated by the physical presence of the bridge and the kinetic sense of moving across it; the last six, having left the "sheened harbor lanterns" behind, remove to a watery element. And as the bridge becomes a symbolic ship, we sense an underlying relaxation. It is true that the language remains rich, even rugged ("Of thy white seizure springs the prophecy"). But the hyperbolic imagery itself seems an effort to substitute verbal energy for genuine tension. The original tension, between the poet-hero and history, seems to be replaced by an unformulated struggle *within* the poet, a struggle to maintain a pitch of language unsupported by a concrete action. For the climactic action of the entire poem had already occurred, when, at the center of the span, the poet names the bridge as "Paradigm." The rest is an effort, bound to prove inadequate in the nature of the case, to say what it is a paradigm of. Thus the poet, full of ponderous (and, we sense, conflicting) emotions, sails away from the harbor, detaching the myth from its concreteness. And the bridge achieves its final transmutation, into a floating and lonely abstraction.

IV

The dissolution of the bridge as fact—and the subsequent drop in the poem's intensity—was perhaps an inevitable outcome of the poet's conflict between his faith and reality. In the summer of 1926, suffering an attack of skepticism about his "myth of America," Crane stated the problem in his own terms. "Intellectually judged," he wrote to Waldo Frank, "the whole theme and project seems more and more absurd." He felt his materials were not authentic, that "these forms, materials, dynamics are simply non-existent in the world." As for Brooklyn Bridge: "The bridge today has no significance beyond an economical approach to shorter hours, quicker lunches, behaviorism and toothpicks." A month later he had recovered his faith. "I feel an absolute music in the air again," he wrote to Frank, "and some tremendous rondure floating somewhere." He had composed the "Proem," in which the bridge stands firmly opposed to the cities. He had beaten back the nightmarish view of the bridge, and could now proceed with his aim of translating a mechanical structure into a threshold of life.[10]

But Crane could not dismiss the nightmare. He had to account for it, and he did so in a subtle fashion. Later in 1926 he arrived at the title for his last section: "Atlantis." Until then, it had been "Bridge Finale." The destination of the protagonist's journey, like Columbus's, had been called Cathay, the traditional symbol of the East. Atlantis was the sunken island of the West—older even than the Orient. What does Crane intend by his new title? Does he mean to identify East and West? Or to introduce the idea of the decline of greatness at the very moment his hero's journey is accomplished? What precisely does Atlantis add to our "cognizance" of the bridge?[11]

---

[10] In light of Crane's efforts to sustain belief in his cultural symbol, Henry Miller's treatment of the bridge is significant. For Miller, Brooklyn Bridge was an intensely private experience—a means of release from his culture. It served him as it did John Marin, as a perspective upon the city. Only Miller found nothing in modern New York to celebrate. "Way up there," he wrote in *Tropic of Capricorn* (Paris, 1939), he seemed to be "hanging over a void": "up there everything that had ever happened to me seemed unreal . . . *unnecessary.*" (p. 72) The bridge, he felt, disconnected him from the "howling chaos" of the shores. See also "The 14th Ward," *Black Spring* (Paris, 1936). In "The Brooklyn Bridge," the concluding essay in *The Cosmological Eye* (New York, 1939), he writes that the bridge had appeared to him with "splendour and illumination" in "violent dreams and visions." He recalled that he took to the bridge "only in moments of extreme anguish," and that he "dreamt very violently" at its center. In these dreams "the whole past would click"; he felt himself annihilated as an ego in space and time, but reborn in a "new realm of consciousness." Thus, he now realizes, the bridge was no longer "a thing of stone and steel" but "incorporated in my consciousness as a symbol." And as a symbol it was a "harp of death," "a means of reinstating myself in the universal stream." Through it he felt "securely situated in my time, yet above it and beyond it." Crane's conception is similar, with this crucial difference: Miller stripped the bridge altogether of its ties with American life, but Crane wished to restore a meaningful relation between bridge and city, and to fuse the personal and the cultural. Moreover, Crane wished to incorporate the stone and steel into the symbol—to join meaning to fact.

Other treatments of the bridge versus the city theme appear in John Dos Passos, *Manhattan Transfer* (New York, 1925); Thomas Wolfe, *The Web and the Rock* (New York, 1938); Vladimir Mayakovsky, "Brooklyn Bridge" (1925), reprinted in *Atlantic* (June 1960); Federico Garcia Lorca, "Unsleeping City (Brooklyn Bridge Nocturne)" (1932), *Poet in New York* (New York, 1955). On May 26, 1923, the Sunday Brooklyn *Eagle* celebrated the fortieth birthday of the bridge with a poem by Martin H. Weyrauch, "The Bridge Speaks," in which the structure argues against modernization of itself in these words: "I think we ought to have/ At least one personality/ In this City of Wild Motion/ That stands for the solid,/ The poised,/ The quiet/ Things of Life." It is likely that Hart Crane, already at work on his poem and living in Brooklyn Heights, read these lines.

[11] In May 1926 Crane recorded in a letter that he had been reading *Atlantis in America* by Lewis Spence. Spence, a leading student of mythology (he died in 1955), devoted much of his time and numerous books to "the At-

The fable of Atlantis had been as important as Cathay to the discovery of the New World. Originally, it was a somewhat mystical legend told by Plato in *Timaeus* and *Critias*, concerning a land in the western ocean (the Atlantic), founded by Poseidon, god of the sea. Once all-powerful, the nation had grown lustful, and was punished for its pride with earthquakes and floods; in a single day it sunk forever. But the legend remained, and during the fifteenth century, was popular among sailors. The island was believed to be the place where seven Portuguese bishops, fleeing the Moors, had founded seven golden cities. Sailors hoped to rediscover this land, where Christians still lived in piety and wealth. To discover Atlantis, or to reach Cathay—these were the leading motifs among the navigators who sailed westward in the fifteenth century. No one, not even Columbus, dreamed that an entirely new world lay between the sunken world and the legendary riches of the Orient.[12]

Crane thus had historical grounds for identifying Atlantis and Cathay. As it turned out, the discovery of America proved both legends to be illusions: neither had the geographical position attributed to it by Renaissance navigators. Both, however, remained active myths—Cathay inspiring the revived theme of the Northwest Passage in the nineteenth century, and Atlantis even yet

---

lantean question." Crane found convincing his argument that there are traces of Atlantean civilization in American Indian culture: "it's easy to believe that a continent existed in mid-Atlantic waters and that the Antilles and West Indies are but salient peaks of its surface" (*Letters*, 255–6). It is, unfortunately, impossible to learn whether Crane knew *Atlantis: The Antediluvian World* (1882)—a remarkable work by Ignatius Donnelly, the fascinating Minnesotan, who tried to found a city in the 1850's, served many years in Congress, was an out-spoken Populist, a Baconian in the controversy over the identity of Shakespeare (he produced a massive argument in 1885, *The Great Cryptogram*), and something of an embittered prophet (*Caesar's Column*, 1890). His book on Atlantis was widely influential among students of the problem; Lewis Spence linked his name with Plato as the most prominent in "Atlantean science." Among the propositions Donnelly tried to prove was that Atlantis was "the true Antediluvian world; the Garden of Eden," and therefore, "the region where man first rose from a state of barbarism to civilization." To establish these—and other—"facts," would, he wrote, "aid us to rehabilitate the fathers of our civilization, our blood, and our fundamental ideas—the men who lived, loved, and labored ages before the Aryans descended upon India, or the Phoenicians had settled in Syria, or the Goths had reached the shores of the Baltic." Atlantis, in other words, provided mankind—and Americans in particular—with a historical tradition far older than any yet imagined. Donnelly's book was reissued, with revisions by Egerton Sykes, in 1949.
[12] See Boies Penrose, *Travel and Discovery in the Renaissance. 1420–1620* (Cambridge, 1952), 5, 19, 25; also, J. H. Parry, *The Age of Reconnaissance* (New York, 1964), 165.

arousing speculation. Crane had indicated early in the composition
of his poem that Cathay would stand for "consciousness, knowledge, spiritual unity"—material conquest transmuted into "an
attitude of spirit." What does Atlantis stand for?

The answer is complex. When we learn from Plato that the
Atlanteans possessed a land with a great central plain, "said to
have been the fairest of all plains, and very fertile," the resemblance to America is striking. Further, we learn that they were a
race of highly inventive builders, who intersected the island with
a vast system of inland canals. They had invented basic tools,
farming, and the alphabet. Their proudest creations, however,
were bridges—a series of bridges, in fact, which led over the canals
toward the exact center of the island. There, a monumental bridge
opened upon the gate to a temple, the shrine of Poseidon.

This was Atlantis in its glory. But, Plato revealed, the glory did
not last. The "divine portion" faded away, and human nature "got
the upper hand." The people grew prideful, avaricious, imperial-
istic. And most of all, they grew blind to their own failings—blind
to the loss of their true powers.

Crane wove references to the sunken island throughout the
fabric of the poem. They appear in "Cutty Sark" as the old sailor's
memory of "the skeletons of cities." They recur forcefully in "The
Tunnel" in two echoes of Poe's "The City in the Sea": "And
Death, aloft,—gigantically down," and "worlds that glow and
sink." And they emerge explicitly in stanza eleven of the finale:

> Now while thy petals spend the suns about us, hold—
> (O Thou whose radiance doth inherit me)
> Atlantis,—hold thy floating singer late!

In the preceding line, the bridge was addressed as a sea creature
—"Anemone." Here, the poet invokes the floating form, now called
Atlantis, to sustain his faith. In the following stanza, the last of
the poem, the poet passes "to thine Everpresence, beyond time,"
as the "orphic strings . . . leap and converge." Then:

> —One Song, one Bridge of Fire! Is it Cathay,
> Now pity steeps the grass and rainbows ring
> The serpent with the eagle in the leaves . . . ?
> Whispers antiphonal in azure swing.

The question *may* indicate doubt that the bridge does in fact represent the "mystic consummation" of Cathay; more likely, it indi-

cates wonder. The antiphonal whispers through the cables of the disembodied bridge could hardly be negative. Atlantis, the bridge-anemone, had answered the prayer and held the "floating singer late."

How did the sunken island earn such a high function? Where did it get the "radiance" to bestow upon the poet? The answer lies once more in Plato's account. The people of Atlantis had indeed become blind in their pride and materialism—but not all of them. "To those who had no eye to see the true happiness, they still appeared glorious and blessed at the very time when they were filled with unrighteous avarice and power." Some, however, retained "an eye to see," and these few recognized baseness as baseness. The still radiant ones kept their "precious gift" of the "divine portion."[13]

It is now clear what Crane meant. His Cathay, his moment of supreme awareness, was a moment of Atlantean "radiance." With an "eye to see," he perceived the bridge as more than stone and steel, as a "mystic consummation." He perceived the gift embodied in the bridge. The inhabitants of the Daemon's dark tunnels could no longer see—no longer make out the shape of the future within the chaos of the present. These are the people for whom the bridge was nothing but "an economical approach." They represented the loss of radiance, the sinking of Atlantis.

Crane used the Atlantis legend, like the epigraph from Job, to maintain a double insight: the promise of redemption and the actuality of evil. As long as he held the double view, as long as he was able to affirm the myth while condemning the actuality of his culture, he would not sink. To this end he required a bridge to rise above the wreckage of history—to rise above itself—and be a pure curveship. The purity was essential; the bridge could harbor no ambiguities. Hence its symbolic radiance became the only enduring fact of Hart Crane's Brooklyn Bridge.

---

[13] It should be noted that Crane's epigraph to "Atlantis" is from *The Symposium:* "Music is then the knowledge of that which relates to love in harmony and system." This reinforces my view of his reliance upon the Platonic version of Atlantis—and the Platonism of *The Bridge.* Harmony and system were central features of the island civilization—as they are of the Platonic cosmology. Love and music, moreover, had been identified with the poet's quest throughout, and with the bridge in "Proem." The image of Atlantis, then, helps Crane draw these threads together in the finale.